SIMMS TO McCONKEY

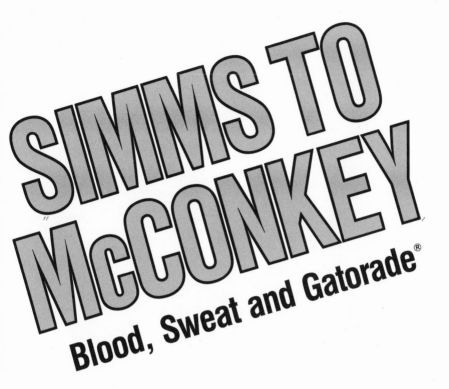

SIMMS TO McCONKEY

Blood, Sweat and Gatorade®

by PHIL McCONKEY
and PHIL SIMMS
of the NEW YORK GIANTS

with Dick Schaap

CROWN PUBLISHERS, INC.
NEW YORK

Copyright © 1987 by Phil Simms, Phil McConkey and Dick Schaap

Published by Crown Publishers, Inc., 225 Park Avenue South, New York, New York 10003 and represented in Canada by the Canadian MANDA Group

CROWN is a trademark of Crown Publishers, Inc.

Manufactured in the United States of America

Library of Congress Cataloging-in-Publication Data
McConkey, Phil.
    Simms to McConkey.

    1. New York Giants (Football team)   2. McConkey, Phil.
3. Simms, Phil.   4. Football players—United States—Biography.
I. Simms, Phil.   II. Schaap, Dick, 1934– .   III. Title.
GV956.N4M43   1987   796.332'64'097471   87-13671
ISBN 0-517-56703-2

10   9   8   7   6   5   4   3   2   1

First Edition

This book is for Bill and Barbara Simms, and for Joe and Jeana McConkey, our parents, and for our brothers and sisters, all of whom nurtured the Super Bowl dream.

This book is for Diana Simms, and for Christopher and Deirdre, who shared the Super Bowl dream.

And this book is for our teammates and coaches, who made the dream a reality.

Contents

CONTENTS

Acknowledgments

First of all, I want to thank Phil Simms for throwing to Phil McConkey, and not Bobby Johnson, on the fleaflicker in the Super Bowl. When I saw that pass completion—*Simms to McConkey*—I cheered in the press box, a gross breach of journalistic etiquette.

Almost twenty years had passed since the last time I cheered in the press box. On December 31, 1967, in Green Bay, Wisconsin, I reacted with similar enthusiasm when Jerry Kramer threw the block that opened the hole for Bart Starr to score the winning touchdown against Dallas in the NFL championship game. CBS Sports then showed the block over and over and over, prompting Kramer to say, "Thank God for *Instant Replay*," which provided the title for *that* book.

I offer my cheers, and thanks, also to Sterling Lord and David Fishof, the odd couple of agents who combined talents to put this book together; to Mark Gompertz, the Crown editor who pursued me and Simms and McConkey all the way to Hollywood to make certain we completed the manuscript almost on time; to Harry Klein, whose research, as always, was thorough and frighteningly well organized; to Al Braverman who, as a lifelong Giants fan, gathered and arranged the accompanying photographs with loving care; and to my wife, Trish, who, even though she was raised in the Scottish Highlands and knows nothing of American football, has learned to cheer for Simms and McConkey and my typing, not necessarily in that order.

—Dick Schaap

Introduction

■ They make an odd couple, Philip Martin Simms and Philip Joseph McConkey of the New York Giants, as similar in some ways as their first names, as different in many ways as their last. They were born less than sixteen months apart, finished their college football careers the same year, and share both a fierce work ethic and a stunningly high threshold of pain.

But Phil Simms plays quarterback, which is the glamour job in professional football, and Phil McConkey runs back punts and kickoffs, which is a dirty job, and also catches passes. Simms, who came to the Giants with great fanfare, is one of the highest-paid members of the team. McConkey, who walked in looking for work, is one of the lowest.

They grew up worlds apart, too, Simms on a family farm in Springfield, Kentucky, the fourth of five sports-minded sons, and McConkey on the inner-city streets of Buffalo, New York, the only son of a vice cop and a feisty woman who tries very hard to teach hard-core juvenile delinquents in a detention facility. (Simms also has three sisters, McConkey one.)

Simms used to toss footballs and baseballs behind the barn. McConkey used to catch passes in the streets, and then, sprinting at full speed, sometimes took awesome hits—from parked cars. He once took a hit from a moving car, found himself flipped in the air, crash-landed and, of course, jumped right up and figuratively shook his fist in the face of the vehicle that had clipped him, as if to say, "Can't you hit any harder than that?"

Simms is tall, six-foot-three, blond and sturdy, 214 pounds, with a face that belongs on a choirboy or a Mississippi raft, a family man, married since the end of his rookie season to the former Diana Fronfield. They have a son, Christopher, who was born in 1980, and a daughter, Deirdre, born in 1984, and they live in a handsome house on an unflinchingly suburban street in Franklin Lakes, New Jersey, a cul-de-sac lined with trees and ten-speed bikes.

McConkey is short, by football standards, not quite the five-foot-ten he and the Giants like to claim, dark-haired and wiry, 165 pounds on a strong day, his cleft chin punctuated by a football scar, a faded purple birthmark next to his right eye, a mustache reinforcing macho good looks. He is a bachelor who, in the dreamlike days after Super Bowl XXI, between commercials, White House visits and televised chats with Dr. Ruth, moved into Manhattan, becoming the only member of the Giants or the Jets to reside in New York City. He sublet a studio apartment just off Broadway that was formerly shared by Alexander Gudonov, the dancer, and Jacqueline Bisset, the actress. He enjoyed telling teammates he was sleeping in Jacqueline Bisset's bed. He did not always mention that she was not there.

Ironically, but not surprisingly, each of them, Simms and McConkey, is to a certain degree envious of the other's role, the other's lifestyle. McConkey dreams of being a star, yet he dreams, too, of settling down, marrying, raising a family in the suburbs. Simms, who has felt the heat of the spotlight, yearns at times for the relative anonymity of a fringe player, and like most of the married men on the Giants, and on the planet, he occasionally fantasizes about what it would be like to be—like McConkey—young, fit, solvent and single. Simms is always asking McConkey about his latest adventure. McConkey lives vicariously, too. He is always asking Simms about his children.

They are good friends, the two Phils, probably each other's closest on the team. Three or four days a week, during the 1986 season, they strained together in the weight room, then unwound together in the steam. Afterward, they sometimes studied game films together. Then, often the last two players to leave Giants Stadium, they drove off in matching his-and-his Corvettes.

They shared the weight room and the steam and the camaraderie with a variety of teammates, but especially with two, Jim Burt, the damaging nose tackle, and Brad Benson, the tackle with the damaged nose. Benson's proboscis is semipermanently scarred and swollen from ramming his helmet into too many chests. Burt has also been accused, by both Simms and McConkey, of absorbing too many heavy blows to the head.

All four love to needle, to rattle each other's cages. Benson, the offensive lineman, insists that he is, at 270 pounds, fleeter of foot than the quarterback he protects. "The great thing about having Phil Simms at quarterback," Benson says, "is that you always know where he is. He doesn't move around. He can't."

Burt swears that the night before the Super Bowl he tiptoed past Simms's hotel room and overheard the quarterback preparing for the most important game of his career by practicing for his post-game commercial. " 'I'm going to Disney World, I'm going to Disney World,' " Burt claims he heard Simms rehearsing. Burt repeated the story gleefully at countless banquets that followed the Super Bowl. "I heard him saying those *three* words over and over," Burt said countless times.

Simms is a frequent target for his teammates, but Mc-

Conkey is the favorite. He takes abuse for his frugal dining habits (he always seems to show up unannounced at the homes of teammates and friends at mealtimes) and for his fickle social habits (he falls in love forever with a different woman each week). McConkey's mother keeps a cardboard box in Buffalo filled with photographs of predominantly shapely women, each of whom, she was once assured, would soon be her daughter-in-law.

His fellow Giants pounce on McConkey, too, for his eagerness to be noticed and appreciated. He won the Dave Jennings Award for the Super Bowl season, an award for self-promotion named after the former Giant who holds the National Football League records for punts in a career and for interviews. Jennings never met a microphone he didn't like. McConkey feels the same way. For him, working on this book was a joy.

Simms is considerably more guarded, more wary, a master of the art of camouflaged conversation, of being open without being revealing. Beware the media as you would beware blitzing linebackers, his coach, Bill Parcells, has warned, and Simms has taken the warning to heart. For him, working on this book was a challenge.

Fortunately, for me, they respond well to challenges, Simms and McConkey, working stiffs both of them, battlers, each always convinced he had abilities that others did not always see. Everyone saw those abilities on January 25, 1987, in Super Bowl XXI, at the Rose Bowl in Pasadena. It was the greatest day of Simms's career. It was the greatest day of McConkey's. This book is the story of the separate but intersecting paths that the two men followed to reach the same peak at the same time.

—*Dick Schaap, 1987*

4

Simms . . .

I've been booed. I've been benched. I've been battered. I've been subjected to every indignity to which a National Football League quarterback can be subjected, except one: I've never been traded. It's not my fault I've never been traded.

I flat begged the New York Giants to trade me in 1983. I begged the Giants to trade me to Houston, New Orleans or Tampa Bay.

But the Giants wouldn't listen to me. They forced me to remain in New York, and three seasons later, while Houston, New Orleans and Tampa Bay all finished dead last in their divisions, the New York Giants—with me playing quarterback—beat the Denver Broncos in Super Bowl XXI.

That victory in the Super Bowl made up for all the boos, the benching and the batterings. Finally, after eight frustrating years for me, and many more for them, I loved all the New York Giants fans, and they all loved me.

I knew they would never boo me again, at least not until our next game.

—Phil Simms, 1987

. . . To McConkey

I knew four years ago I'd score a touchdown in the Super Bowl. I knew it the day my friend Kit McCulley and I marked off 40 yards on the street in front of his house in Pensacola, Florida, and I ran the 40 yards as fast as I could, and Kit clicked the stopwatch and looked down and said, "Whew!"

I was a twenty-six-year-old lieutenant in the U.S. Navy, a helicopter pilot by training. After four years away from football, I was going to try out for the New York Giants, and I'd been told that, to have even a slight chance, I had to run 40 yards in four-point-six seconds or less.

"What was it?" I said.

"Four-point-four-eight," Kit said.

We went out and celebrated. We drank margaritas and talked and, by the second margarita, we knew that I'd make the New York Giants, the Giants would make the Super Bowl, I'd score a touchdown to help win the Super Bowl, and then, because the odds against me were so great, I'd write a book about it.

We were just dreaming, of course, but all the dreams came true.

—*Phil McConkey, 1987*

McConkey on Simms

Phil Simms is the toughest man on the Giants, physically and mentally. No one takes so many vicious hits, on the field and off, and keeps getting up.

No quarterback stands in so long, looking for an opening. He doesn't have jittery feet. He doesn't have jittery thoughts. He doesn't care if he has 275 pounds of defensive lineman in his face. He'd rather be hammered then hurried.

He's been blind-sided, clothes-lined and cracked-back, by the public and by the press—if I had a nickel for every time I heard somebody bad-mouth him, I'd be a rich man—and yet he's almost always polite and cooperative with both.

Most guys would've folded under the punishment he's taken, but he's just gotten mentally and physically tougher. He's the kind of guy who always thinks he can beat you, at anything.

No one's more popular with his teammates, for his skill and courage and generosity. He gave his offensive line, his blockers, television sets one year, and portraits of themselves another year. The linemen fight to go out to dinner with him because they know he'll pick up the tab.

The best thing I can say about Phil Simms is: He's the quarterback every lineman would love to be.

Simms on McConkey

Phil McConkey is the youngest man on the Giants, not in years, but in spirit. He's like a little kid on the field, he loves being a football player so much. He loves running down the sidelines. He loves doing calisthenics. I think he even loves getting hit.

He's so emotional. He laughs on the field. He shouts. He cries. He gets frustrated and he gets angry and he gets even. He's into the game every minute. He's the symbol of our intensity and our enthusiasm, but he's much more than just a symbol.

He's an athlete. He has speed, exceptional speed, more than he's given credit for. He has quickness. He has remarkable hand-and-eye coordination. He has athletic instincts and athletic intelligence, and he is absolutely fearless. Every catch he makes for us is a killer. He doesn't care. He'll play in pain. He wears scars and bruises like decorations.

Of course, like most of us, he's a little kid off the field, too. He loves meeting famous people. He loves meeting beautiful women. He loves recognition and attention, and he loves being a special part of something special.

I guess the thing about Phil McConkey is: He really loves being Phil McConkey.

Phil McConkey's Credo

■ Wide receiver Fred Biletnikoff of the Oakland Raiders, the Most Valuable Player in Super Bowl XI, was once asked what it was like to make a big catch in the biggest game. "It's almost as good as having sex," he replied.

Biletnikoff's remark was passed along to Phil McConkey after the little Giant made two big catches in Super Bowl XXI. "I'll remember those two plays the rest of my life," McConkey said. "I don't know if I've had a sexual experience I'll remember the rest of my life."

"Are you saying Biletnikoff's wrong?" McConkey was asked.

"Oh no," McConkey said. "I'm just saying he's had better sex than I've had."

THE NEW YORK GIANTS OF SUPER BOWL XXI

January 25, 1987

No.	Name	Pos.	Ht.	Wt.	Age	College
Inj.	Adams, George	RB	6-1	225	24	Kentucky
2	Allegre, Raul	K	5-10	167	27	Texas
24	Anderson, Ottis	RB	6-2	225	29	Miami
67	Ard, Billy	G	6-3	270	27	Wake Forest
58	Banks, Carl	LB	6-4	235	24	Michigan State
89	Bavaro, Mark	TE	6-4	245	23	Notre Dame
60	Benson, Brad	T	6-3	270	31	Penn State
64	Burt, Jim	NT	6-1	260	27	Miami
53	Carson, Harry	LB	6-2	240	33	So. Carolina State
44	Carthon, Maurice	RB	6-1	225	25	Arkansas State
25	Collins, Mark	CB	5-10	190	22	Cal State–Fullerton
Inj.	Davis, Tyrone	CB	6-1	190	25	Clemson
77	Dorsey, Eric	DE	6-5	280	22	Notre Dame
28	Flynn, Tom	S	6-0	195	24	Pittsburgh
30	Galbreath, Tony	RB	6-0	225	32	Missouri
61	Godfrey, Chris	G	6-3	265	28	Michigan
54	Headen, Andy	LB	6-5	242	26	Clemson
48	Hill, Kenny	S	6-0	195	28	Yale
Inj.	Hostetler, Jeff	QB	6-3	215	25	West Virginia
74	Howard, Erik	NT	6-4	268	22	Washington State
57	Hunt, Byron	LB	6-5	242	28	Southern Methodist
88	Johnson, Bobby	WR	5-11	171	25	Kansas
68	Johnson, Damian	T	6-5	290	24	Kansas State
52	Johnson, Pepper	LB	6-3	248	22	Ohio State
59	Johnston, Brian	C	6-3	275	24	North Carolina
51	Jones, Robbie	LB	6-2	230	27	Alabama
Inj.	Jordan, David	G	6-6	275	24	Auburn
Inj.	Kinard, Terry	S	6-1	200	27	Clemson
5	Landeta, Sean	P	6-0	200	24	Towson State
46	Lasker, Greg	S	6-0	200	22	Arkansas
86	Manuel, Lionel	WR	5-11	175	24	Pacific
70	Marshall, Leonard	DE	6-3	285	25	Louisiana State

75	Martin, George	DE	6-4	255	33	Oregon
80	McConkey, Phil	WR	5-10	170	29	Navy
Inj.	McGriff, Curtis	DE	6-5	276	28	Alabama
87	Miller, Solomon	WR	6-1	185	22	Utah State
20	Morris, Joe	RB	5-7	195	26	Syracuse
84	Mowatt, Zeke	TE	6-3	240	25	Florida State
63	Nelson, Karl	T	6-6	285	26	Iowa State
65	Oates, Bart	C	6-3	265	28	Brigham Young
34	Patterson, Elvis	CB	5-11	188	26	Kansas
55	Reasons, Gary	LB	6-4	234	24	N.W. Louisiana State
66	Roberts, William	T	6-5	280	24	Ohio State
81	Robinson, Stacy	WR	5-11	186	24	North Dakota State
22	Rouson, Lee	RB	6-1	222	24	Colorado
17	Rutledge, Jeff	QB	6-1	195	29	Alabama
78	Sally, Jerome	NT	6-3	270	27	Missouri
11	Simms, Phil	QB	6-3	214	31	Morehead State
56	Taylor, Lawrence	LB	6-3	243	27	North Carolina
Inj.	Washington, John	DE	6-4	275	23	Oklahoma State
27	Welch, Herb	S	5-11	180	25	UCLA
23	Williams, Perry	CB	6-3	203	25	North Carolina State

COACHES

Name	Title	College
Bill Parcells	Head coach	Wichita State
Bill Belichick	Defensive coordinator	Wesleyan
Romeo Crennel	Special teams	Western Kentucky
Ron Erhardt	Offensive coordinator	Jamestown
Len Fontes	Defensive backfield	Ohio State
Ray Handley	Running backs	Stanford
Fred Hoaglin	Offensive line	Pittsburgh
Pat Hodgson	Receivers	Georgia
Lamar Leachman	Defensive line	Tennessee
Johnny Parker	Strength and conditioning	Mississippi
Mike Pope	Tight ends	Lenoir-Rhyne
Mike Sweatman	Assistant special teams	Kansas

BLOOD

1979–1982

■ Jeana McConkey, the teenaged wife of teenaged Joe McConkey, was seven months pregnant with their first child, whom they would call Phil, when the New York Giants won the championship of the National Football League for the fourth time in their history and for the last time until Super Bowl XXI. Phil Simms was in his Kentucky crib, not quite fourteen months old.

The date was December 30, 1956.

The score was 47–7.

The opponents were the Chicago Bears.

The Giants' lineup was magnificent, with old Charlie Conerly at quarterback and rookie Sam Huff at linebacker, with Alex Webster, Frank Gifford and Kyle Rote all scoring touchdowns.

That was the first of eight consecutive memorable seasons for the Giants and their fans, seasons in which they won more than 70 percent of their 102 regular-season games and won their division championship six times. They were truly Giants, and nine of them—tackle Roosevelt Brown, halfback Gifford, linebacker Huff, offensive coach Vince Lombardi, owner Tim Mara, head coach Steve Owen, end Andy Robustelli, quarterback Y. A. Tittle and safety Emlen Tunnell—were elected to the Professional Football Hall of Fame.

The only blemish on their handsome record was the fact that, after the one-sided victory over Chicago, the Giants lost their next five NFL championship games, two to the Baltimore Colts (one in a thrilling sudden-death overtime game that helped lift pro football to a new level), two to the Green Bay Packers (who were coached by the former Giant assistant, Vince Lombardi) and one to the Chicago Bears.

After the Bears came from behind to win the NFL title, 14–10, on December 29, 1963—Tittle passed to Gifford for the first touchdown of the game—the Giants embarked on a downward course that was spectacularly noted, at the final home game in 1978, when a small plane circled over Giants Stadium towing a sign that said, 15 YRS. OF LOUSY FOOTBALL —WE'VE HAD ENOUGH.

Wellington Mara, the president of the Giants, was hanged in effigy that day, and in the parking lots of the stadium, the traditional site of tailgate parties, Giant tickets were symbolically barbecued.

During those fifteen lousy years, the Giants managed to produce only two winning seasons, neither of which qualified the team for the playoffs. In six of those fifteen futile seasons, the Giants won only three or fewer games, and in 1978, the false hopes raised by five victories in the first eight games were promptly dashed by the disappointing reality of a six-game losing streak. The most horrendous of those six defeats took place in November, in Giants Stadium, against the Philadelphia Eagles.

The Giants were winning, 17–12, in the closing seconds. The Giants had the ball. The Eagles had no time-outs remaining. All the Giants' quarterback, Joe Pisarcik, had to do was take the snap from center, collapse on the ball, watch the clock run out, then celebrate the victory. Instead, Pisarcik was instructed to hand off to fullback Larry Csonka, and when the handoff misfired into a fumble, Philadelphia's Herman Edwards pounced on the loose ball and raced for a touchdown that beat the Giants and branded them.

The play became known, for at least as long as witnesses live, as The Fumble, recalled by Giant fans as warmly as the surviving citizens of Pompeii remembered The Eruption. The spirit of The Fumble persisted until Super Bowl XXI, a spirit that made every Giant fan, loyal member of an abused species, expect each promising moment to turn to disaster.

Phil McConkey and Phil Simms were in their final fall of college football when The Fumble struck.

Alex Webster had served as the Giants' head coach in the middle of the fifteen forlorn years, Andy Robustelli as the general manager at the end. But the fact that their names conjured up images of the team's brilliant past only underscored the dreariness of the present. Clearly, the Giants needed drastic change.

But the co-owners of the team, Wellington Mara and his young nephew, Tim, the team's vice-president, could not agree on how to effect change. The nephew, in fact, attempted a coup. He sought to oust his uncle and seize control of the foundering organization. Tim Mara's plot failed, but the two men stopped speaking to each other, and have never resumed.

Pete Rozelle, the commissioner of the NFL, spoke to both of the feuding Maras and persuaded them to annoint, as their general manager, a man neither of them knew, a former secondary-school teacher of history and political science.

On Valentine's Day, 1979, George Young became the general manager of the Giants. Once a Little All-American at Bucknell, Young had spent eleven years absorbing the history and politics of pro football with the Baltimore Colts and the Miami Dolphins. He was offensive coordinator of the Colts, director of personnel and pro scouting for the Dolphins.

Young chose Ray Perkins, an Alabama man, then an assistant with the San Diego Chargers, to become the eleventh head coach in the history of the Giants. Perkins and Young decided that their first priority, if they were to rebuild the franchise that old Tim Mara, a bookmaker by trade, had purchased in 1925 for a few hundred dollars, was to find a quarterback, a young man who could be both the symbol and the substance of the future.

They chose Phil Simms.

1979

In which Simms gets drafted,
and McConkey gets commissioned

CONKS We were cutting across one of the athletic fields at Annapolis, three or four of us midshipmen, walking to the dock to go out on a YP, a yard patrol, a mini-destroyer that we used for training at the Naval Academy. One of the guys was looking at the sports pages of the paper. "You see this?" he said. "The New York Giants drafted a quarterback from some school called Morehead State College in the first round. What a joke! Somebody named Phil Simms."

SIMMS I was the seventh player drafted in the whole country. I was the second quarterback. Jack Thompson of Washington State University was picked ahead of me. He was picked by the Cincinnati Bengals. He was called "The Throwin' Samoan." I was called Phil Simms.

CONKS "Look at this," the guy who was reading the paper said. "There were a bunch of Giants fans at the draft and they booed when they picked Simms. 'Phil who?' they said. They never even heard of him.''

I'd heard of Phil Simms. I studied the sports pages. I read everything about football. I even knew Morehead State College was somewhere in Kentucky.

SIMMS I went to Morehead State because I was slow and skinny when I got out of Southern High School in Louisville. Besides, I missed half my senior season with a separated shoulder. I did come back in time to help us get to the state finals, but still, Morehead was the only place that offered me a full scholarship.

Morehead State was in the Ohio Valley Conference, playing schools like Marshall and Western Kentucky. We didn't win too often. We never had a winning season while I was at Morehead. One year we did start off two-and-one, but we ended up two-and-eight.

I didn't make the All–Ohio Valley team my senior year, mostly because we didn't pass as much as we did my junior year. My junior year, I passed often enough and good enough to make honorable-mention All-American in *The Sporting News*.

CONKS I defended Phil Simms. "I bet you he makes it," I said. "Those people know what they're doing in the draft. They make mistakes, but they don't make mistakes in the first round. They know a hell of a lot more than we do."

SIMMS The NFL knew all about me. More than a dozen different teams sent coaches and scouts to Morehead to work me out, to see if I could throw.

I could throw. I could always throw. A football or a baseball. It just came natural to me. My daddy could throw, too.

Bill Walsh, the San Francisco coach, came down to Morehead himself to watch me throw. "I just want you to throw nice and soft," he told me. "Make it float. Make it pretty. I want to see good rhythm."

Then Ray Perkins, the Giants' coach, came to look at me, and when I saw him, I couldn't believe he was a coach in the NFL. He was wearing black coaching shoes, no socks, shorts and glasses, and he was unbelievably skinny. He'd had the Giant job for just a few weeks, and he'd been killing himself, never sleeping.

"Coach, how do you want me to throw the ball?" I said.

"Son," Perkins said, "I want you to throw that ball as hard as you can every time."

"Even the short passes?" I said.

"I want you to knock 'em down," he said.

I was pretty strong by then. I'd been lifting weights since the end of my senior year in high school. I had six of the guys who'd played with me at Morehead catching passes, and I just threw as hard as I could till they couldn't run anymore.

"Men, just stand out there," Perkins said. "You don't have to run no more. Phil, drop back and throw it. Knock 'em down."

I just kept throwing.

Afterward, Perkins took me for a bite to eat, and we chatted for a while, and when he dropped me off, I said, "Coach, it was nice meeting you," and he said, "Son, you're going to have a great career in the National Football League."

He called me a few days later and asked me what I thought about becoming a New York Giant, and I said I thought it'd be great. In all honesty, I didn't want to, but I didn't tell him that. I knew the Giants didn't have a strong team, but that had nothing to do with it. It was just that I'd grown up in the East, and I'd never really traveled, I'd never even been on an airplane, and I really thought it'd be great to go out to the West Coast, maybe San Francisco or San Diego, I didn't care which.

Coach Walsh came back to Morehead, worked me out for

a second time, then told me, "Phil, you're going to be the leading passer in pro football every year." He also told me the 49ers were going to make me their first draft choice. They didn't have a pick in the first round, but they had the first pick in the second round. I told Coach Walsh I didn't think I was going to last that long, that other teams had told me they were going to draft me in the first round. "Don't worry about that," he said. "We've checked with everybody. You'll be there."

I wasn't. The Giants took me, and the 49ers didn't draft a quarterback till the third round. They picked Joe Montana from Notre Dame. Everybody had heard of him and his school.

CONKS I wanted to see where Joe Montana went in the draft. He and I played together in the Japan Bowl in Tokyo a few months before the draft. I figured that was the last football game I was ever going to play in.

I had an obligation to spend five years in the United States Navy after I got my commission. That was why nobody in the NFL drafted me. Nobody spent five years in the navy and then made it in the NFL. Nobody except Roger Staubach, and he was a Heisman Trophy winner. He was a legend.

SIMMS The day of the draft, my parents and I set up head-quarters at the Holiday Inn in Morehead. We didn't have to wait long before the Giants called to say they'd drafted me in the first round. Once they called, I stopped thinking about the West Coast. I was perfectly happy to be going to the Giants. They didn't tell me about the booing at the draft.

They said they'd been through some rough years, but with Ray Perkins and George Young they were going to turn it around, and I was going to be a part of it. They said I was going to be a big part of it.

For the first time in my life, I started thinking about the

Super Bowl. Up till then, my only dream had been to win the championship of the Ohio Valley Conference.

CONKS I'd been dreaming about the Super Bowl almost my whole life. I grew up in Buffalo, New York, and I lived and died with the Bills. They had great teams in the sixties, great players like Jack Kemp at quarterback and Cookie Gilchrist at running back and Elbert "Golden Wheels" Dubenion at wide receiver. I used to pretend I was all three of them.

Most of the time I pretended to be Kemp and Dubenion, both at once. I'd be Kemp and I'd throw the ball, and then I'd be Dubenion and I'd dive for the ball. I'd do it in the house, throw the ball and then dive on the couch to catch it, or on the bed or on the floor, and I'd do it outside, dive in a snowbank for the ball. I always had a ball in my hand and I was always throwing it up and then catching it, usually diving for it. I loved to make diving catches.

The Bills won the championship of the American Football League in 1964 and 1965, and even though I was only nine years old, it broke my heart when the Kansas City Chiefs beat them in the title game in 1966. The Chiefs went on to play the Green Bay Packers in Super Bowl I, and I started dreaming about the day I'd be playing for the Bills and we'd go to the Super Bowl and I'd make a diving catch for a touchdown. I saw it happen a thousand times.

SIMMS I always figured I'd play ball for a living. Some kind of ball. Probably baseball. My grandfather loved baseball, and when we lived on his farm in Springfield, he used to take his vacation during spring training and go down to Florida and watch the major-league teams work out.

My dad loved baseball, too. He and my mom took their honeymoon in Cincinnati, during a homestand for the Reds, so that they could go to the games.

My dad wanted to be a baseball player, and so did I. In

Little League, I was a terror. Whitey Simms. I could strike out everybody and I could hit the ball over the fence. I hit three over the fence in one game once, and I was really proud of that, and when I came home, my mom said, "How'd you do?"

"I did pretty good," I said. "I hit three home runs."

She got all excited, and I couldn't wait till she told my dad, and when she did, he turned to me and said, "Well, did you hit 'em good, son, or did you pop 'em up?"

"I hit line drives, Dad," I said, "just like you want me to."

I didn't realize till later that he called me "son" when he approved of what I'd done, and he called me "boy" when he didn't.

I always wanted his approval, but he didn't give it too easily because he didn't want me to get lazy. He didn't want me to get into bad habits. Sometimes he'd tell my mom, "You know, that little boy can play his ass off," but he'd just tell me, "You played pretty good, son."

I still pitched and played the outfield in high school and in American Legion ball, and when I was seventeen, I played in a Legion tournament in North Carolina. It was the first time I'd ever been out of Kentucky, except just to cross over to Indiana.

If any major-league baseball team had drafted me out of high school and offered me any kind of contract, I probably would have jumped at it. I probably never would have gone to college, never would have played professional football.

CONKS There was no way I was not going to college. My father was going to see to that. He'd been a football player, too. He played at Lafayette High School in Buffalo, and he was good enough to win a partial scholarship to Colgate University. But he had taken a job working construction, making good money, and he was going out with my mother at the time, so he decided not to go to college.

They got married when they were nineteen, and I got there the next year, and my sister Debbie arrived three years later. My father worked construction for ten years, and then he became a detective on the Buffalo police force, but he always held another job, working security or something like that, to make enough money to support the family. He knew not going to college was a mistake, and he wasn't going to let me make the same mistake. He pumped school into my head.

He sent me to a Catholic grammar school—I was an altar boy, I knew the whole Mass inside out, I even thought I might want to become a priest—and then he sent me to Canisius, which was a Jesuit high school. I would have been perfectly happy to go to Lafayette, like he and my mother and most of the kids in my neighborhood did, but he thought I'd learn more at Canisius. He scraped up the money for it. He wouldn't let me work part time or even during the summers. He wanted me to work just on my studies and sports. He thought they were both very important.

SIMMS I always worked. I remember on the farm, I couldn't have been more than five or six, I used to walk along behind our old tractor, keeping my hands on the suspension chair and looking down to make sure my dad, when he was weeding, didn't cover up any of the tobacco plants.

It was a big farm, a couple of hundred acres, with corn and tobacco and sheep and cattle and hogs and chickens. We always had plenty to eat. We'd get up early, eat breakfast, work awhile, then around ten-thirty or eleven eat a big meal, just eat like crazy. That's what farmers do, they don't have a whole lot of other pleasures. I think that's why I've got the appetite I've got today.

My dad worked hard on the farm, and he felt that my grandfather, his father, should have turned the farm over to him while he was young enough to work hard and enjoy it. But my grandfather wouldn't let go, and they had a big fight over it, and when I was about eight or nine, we moved off the farm and into Louisville. My mom and dad both went to work in a tobacco factory.

I guess my dad and his dad made up, because I remember my grandfather always used to come to visit us. The interesting thing was that my dad's dad was married to my mom's mom. His wife had died early, and her husband had died early, and they had gotten married. I don't know whether they got married before my folks did, or after. I never thought to ask and both my grandparents died before I got out of college.

Between working in the tobacco factory and raising eight children, my mom and dad didn't get too much rest. I always wanted to help, always felt that I had to work. I laid blacktop for a couple of summers, which is brutal work, and I painted houses for $100 a house, which makes you paint fast, and I loaded liquor for one of the Kentucky distillers. The best-paying job I had, the summer before my senior year at Morehead, was on the assembly line at the Ford plant, helping to put trucks together. I was getting seven or eight dollars an hour, working sixty hours a week, grossing about $500 a week, which I thought was all the money in the world.

My job was to put steel cables in the chassis and then bolt them down so that the next guy could do his job. It wasn't a hard job if you knew what you were doing, but at the beginning, I didn't. They gave me about three minutes of instruction and that was it, and then sent me out on the line. There were different types of cables for each truck, and by the time I'd get one bolted down, the next truck would be coming along and I'd run to look for the right cable and sometimes I'd grab the wrong one and I'd sweat and be nervous and every once in a while I'd miss one, let one get by me, and I knew I'd catch hell.

"Boy, you missed one," the foreman would tell me.

"Yes, sir."

"You like working here, boy?"

"Yes, sir."

"You miss one more, boy, and I'll fire your ass."

"Yes, sir."

Eventually I got better at it, but the first couple of weeks were hell. I said to myself, "God bless education, because I know, no matter what happens, I'm going to get a job that beats this."

CONKS I was always a good athlete. But I wasn't the best in the neighborhood. Patty Raimondo was the best. He ended up playing baseball in the Los Angeles Dodgers organization, but he could play anything. Teach him a game, and he'd play it once or twice, and then he'd beat you. Patty was smaller than me, too. We lived in an Italian neighborhood—my mother's Sicilian and my father's half Italian and half Scottish—and we had a lot of small, tough kids.

I wasn't the toughest kid in the neighborhood, either. I had a friend named Vinnie who was really tough. Once, when we were about thirteen years old, a gang of young Puerto Rican kids came marching into our neighborhood. There must have been thirty of them. A kid named Julio was in front. He had a metal chain wrapped around one hand and he was slapping it against the other.

Julio and his gang moved toward us, and I started to back up. I knew if I had a six-yard head start, I could outrun anybody. But Vinnie didn't move. He just stood there, staring. Julio stopped right in front of Vinnie, maybe a foot away from him, and I backed up a little more. Vinnie didn't move. Then he spit in Julio's face.

I couldn't believe it. I was ready to flee, and Vinnie still didn't move. Julio began to wind up with the chain, and Vinnie stood there, and then, as Julio swung, Vinnie ducked, shot his right arm straight in the air, let the chain wrap itself around his arm, then jerked the other end out of Julio's hand and slashed him across the face with it. Julio's face splattered, and I took off. Vinnie waited a few seconds. Then he took off, too. We both escaped without a scratch.

We did wild things, growing up in Buffalo. We raced our bikes through the grounds of a local mental institution, imagining the worst. We rode rafts down the Niagara River, toward the Falls, daring each other to float deeper into the rapids. At night, in the winter, when ice covered the streets, we grabbed the backs of cars and hitched slippery rides. We also used to hop aboard freight trains and ride for a mile or two to the customary stop on the outskirts of Buffalo. Once the train didn't stop, didn't even slow down for more than twenty miles. One of the guys had to call his father to come and get us; I never told my father about that.

But we put most of our time and energy into sports. I weighed less than seventy pounds when I played midget football in a league where the limit was 105. I played in the streets, too, and thought nothing of diving onto the hood of a parked car to make a catch. I was tough. I was Golden Wheels McConkey.

SIMMS I threw my first official pass for the sixth-grade team at St. Rita's School in Louisville. I hit David Grakul for 60 yards and a touchdown. David was the son of our coach, Julian Grakul. Mr. Grakul told my dad that I was going to be a football player some day. My dad didn't believe him. My dad thought I was too small ever to be a football player.

My dad played high school football in Springfield. He played guard, and he played with a bad knee, with loose cartilage, that he used to wrap in an Ace bandage. He was the first player in his league to wear a face mask, a big iron face mask. He said he had to wear it after somebody stepped on his face.

Bear Bryant wanted my dad to come up to Lexington to try out for the University of Kentucky, but my dad said no, thanks, he'd had enough football in high school. More than forty years later, his knee still hurts him.

Somebody talked my dad into coming to see our sixth-grade championship game. It was wet and cold, and he didn't want to go, but he did, and he told some other people that he was amazed by what he saw. He couldn't believe I could throw a football that well.

Of course, he never told me that. He didn't want me to get a big head.

CONKS When I entered Canisius High School, I couldn't wait to go out for the football team. But a couple of days before the first practice, my grandfather came to the house and brought us a lemon meringue pie and some pickled tomatoes, and I ate them both together and I got sick, too sick to go to practice.

My father went instead the first day and walked up to one of the assistant coaches and said that he had a son who was a pretty good football player. My father said that I was sick and that he wanted to make certain I got a fair chance when I recovered. "He's a player," my father said.

"How big is your boy?" the coach asked.

"He's about one hundred and twenty pounds," my father said.

The coach looked at him. "Oh, we get a lot of one-hundred-and-twenty-pound All-Americans here," he said.

My father came home and told me not to worry about my size. "With heart and guts," he said, "you can be ten feet tall."

I was one of only two sophomores who made the Canisius varsity.

Sometimes I don't know how I ever got through football or studies or anything in high school. I was always thinking about girls. I'd be on my way to play a pickup game of basketball with the guys, and if we passed a group of girls, the other guys would shield me from them. Because they knew if I saw the girls, I'd go with them instead of playing basketball.

SIMMS It was different for me. I'd rather play a pickup game of basketball than . . .

CONKS Than what?

SIMMS Than most anything.

CONKS Once my hormones kicked in, that was all I could think about. I'd be on a bus, going to a game, and I'd think of sex, and I'd get a hard-on.

SIMMS I always thought about the game. I was shy, especially with girls.

CONKS We had a beautiful chapel at Canisius High, and every week, before we played, I went to the chapel, all dressed for the game except for my shoulder pads and jersey, and I prayed. "Just let us win one more time," I told God, "and if we keep winning, and I do well, then I'll be able to get into a good college and I'll get a good education and I'll be able to do good things to help other people. I'll pay You back, I promise You. Just let us win one more."

We didn't lose a game the three years I played for Canisius. By the time I graduated, I figured I owed Him a lot. I was never going to forget that, and I knew He wasn't going to, either.

Canisius didn't lose a game the three years after I graduated, too, but somebody else owes Him for that, not me.

I obviously wasn't a born football player. I had to work to be one. In the winter, when the snow would pile up over the curb and freeze, I'd run along the top ledge, on sheer ice, run as fast as I could, then try to make sharp cuts on the ice. I fell down a lot, but I improved my balance, too. I also did things like dribble the football so that no matter what kind of weird hop it took, I'd be able to grab it, and bounce the football off my shoulders and chest and head so that I'd be able to recover quickly and catch bobbled balls. I studied the game.

I never missed a game in high school, not even the time I got hit by a car. The car was going thirty to thirty-five miles an hour and hit me broadside, a clean shot, and I somersaulted off my bicycle and landed on the hood of the car and got a short ride before the woman who was driving was able to jam on the brakes. I bounced right up and tried to get back on my bike, but it was mangled beyond repair. I missed two days of practice, that's all.

I played just about every minute of every game at Canisius, flanker on offense and cornerback on defense, punt returner and kickoff returner, leading the team in receptions and interceptions, without any rest. My senior year, I was the only guy on the team playing both ways, and at the end of every game I'd be physically sick, I was so tired. The other guys would go out to celebrate, and I'd go home with a fever and throw up.

I made All–Western New York on offense and I made All–New York State on defense. I had good grades, too, a B-to-B-plus average, but still the Notre Dames and the Michigans and the Penn States didn't come recruiting me. I only weighed 145 pounds as a senior. The Ivy League schools were interested, and so were Lehigh and Bucknell and Rochester Institute of Technology and the service academies, Army and Navy. The University of Kentucky sent me a form letter, just to see if I was interested in going there.

Eventually it came down to Army and Navy, mostly as a matter of economics. You not only got full scholarships to those places, you also got paid for going to school. I didn't want to be a drain on my family anymore. I visited both Annapolis and West Point. At Army, the coaches showed me around. At Navy, the midshipmen escorted me. That impressed me. I decided to go to the Naval Academy. Besides, I thought I'd look bigger in white.

If I'd picked West Point, I'd probably still be in the army now, probably be a captain, bucking for major.

The worst thing about going away to college was leaving my girlfriend. Her name was Connie McQuestion. She was short and dark and athletic, a cheerleader at Nardin Academy, which was the sister school to Canisius.

I'd gone out with other girls, but Connie was my first real relationship. It was serious. She called my mother and father Mom and Dad.

I thought I was going to marry her.

■ Phil McConkey formed several enduring friendships in his four years at the United States Naval Academy, the first and most durable with a classmate named Kit McCulley, a quarterback from Annapolis High School. McCulley was McConkey's direct link to professional football.

Kit's father, Pete McCulley, once an assistant coach at Navy, worked for the Baltimore Colts when Phil and Kit were plebes, spent the next two seasons as an assistant coach with the Washington Redskins, then, when Phil and Kit were seniors, became head coach of the San Francisco 49ers. Pete McCulley once held all the passing records at Louisiana Tech —till Terry Bradshaw came along.

McConkey met McCulley during their plebe summer, the indoctrination period preceding their first school year. They were teammates in a touch football game. "Throw me the ball," McConkey said, the first time they spoke. "I can beat those guys."

"He weighed about 145 pounds," McCulley recalls, "and even then he had the confidence he could succeed on any level."

1 9 7 9

McConkey and McCulley were among a small fleet of midshipmen adopted, for the undergraduate duration, by Glo and Hank George, one of many Annapolis couples who volunteered to "sponsor" Naval Academy students, to provide them with a sense of home away from home. They gave McConkey a key to their house, and as far as they know, he still has it.

One Christmas, his fellow adoptees designated McConkey to purchase a present for the Georges. The gift was a lovely cut-glass bowl, which McConkey proudly presented, wrapped by his own hands, in cheerful Christmas paper secured with black masking tape.

When McConkey bought his first car in the spring of his junior year, he kept the shining Corvette at the Georges' home. He took the blanket off his bed at Bancroft Hall and put it over the car, which he felt needed to be protected more than he did.

Of course, the Georges shared McConkey's social life. They recall that he dated, among others, a cheerleader, a Barbara I, a Barbara II, and a female midshipman who was known admiringly as Treasure Chest.

"We referred to Phil's women as 'stats,' " Mrs. George remembers.

In 1987, McConkey invited Kit McCulley and Glo and Hank George to be his guests at Super Bowl XXI.

CONKS I never would've made it to the Naval Academy without my parents' sacrifices, and I never would have made it through without their support. The first year and a half at Annapolis, I cried every night, I hated it so much. I hated the regimentation, the loneliness, the difficulty of the classwork. I missed Buffalo, my friends, the neighborhood. I missed Connie so much.

Once I called my mother, Jeana—she had started college

herself at night, at Buffalo State—and I told her how miserable I was, and she told me to come home. My father took the phone from her and screamed at her and told me there was no way I was coming home, no way I was quitting. I was going to get the education he had never gotten. I was going to stick it out.

I did.

SIMMS I wasn't a bad student in college—I went to classes most of the time—but I was a great gambler. I loved to hang out in the pool hall, shoot a little pool, play a little Ping-Pong, win a little money. I hustled.

I met one of my best friends that way. Larry Sloane. He was a few years older than me. He'd played baseball at Morehead, dropped out for a while, then come back. He was a good little athlete, a good little gambler, too. We kept passing our money back and forth till we realized we were wasting valuable time playing each other. We could beat anybody else.

Larry teaches now at the University of Mississippi, and when we see each other, we still go at it, golf, gin rummy, anything. I still want to beat him just as bad as I did in college.

I still see John Moses, too, who was my center at Morehead and probably my best friend. Just by coincidence, when John moved to Louisville a few years ago, he ended up moving in with Rick Nall, who was my best friend from high school.

John and Rick are both bachelors, and every now and then they come up to New Jersey to visit with me.

CONKS We had good football teams while I was at Navy. We had an All-American defensive back, Chet Moeller, who was a couple of years ahead of me. He weighed 185 pounds and hit so hard he used to break tackling dummies. We beat Army three times during my four years at Annapolis. I played only offense. They figured I was too small to play defense in college.

My sophomore year, I made a diving catch for a touchdown against Army, and pictures of the catch ended up in newspapers all over the country. My junior year, I caught thirty-four passes and averaged more than 13 yards per punt return, the second-best average in the nation, behind Jimmy Cefalo of Penn State. My senior year, we won our first seven games, then lost to Notre Dame.

In our next game, against Syracuse, I signaled for a fair catch, but one of their guys hit me anyway and smashed up my knee. Joe Morris told me years later that their coach at Syracuse had said they had to take me out of the game—I think he meant keep the ball away from me—and the guy who made the tackle took the coach's words literally. He took me out of the game.

I had a second-degree sprain, and the doctors thought seriously about operating. Fortunately, they decided not to. I sat out the last two games of the regular season, but I still got All-American honorable mention and I recovered in time to play in the first Holiday Bowl, in San Diego, against Brigham Young University.

Marc Wilson and Jim McMahon were the quarterbacks for BYU, and they had us down, 16–3. But we came back and beat them, 23–16. I scored the winning touchdown on a 65-yard pass play. I also caught three other passes and gained 42 yards rushing on two reverses. I was five-foot-ten and 163 pounds, but the *San Diego Union* said I was "the biggest man on the field." I won the Most Valuable Player award.

I enjoyed my last two years at Annapolis, except for the knee injury and one other thing. Midway through my junior year, Connie broke up with me. She was back home in Buffalo, and she met someone else, and I was heartbroken, I was sick. I cried.

Connie got married a couple of years later.

We're still friends. She works with my mother at Father Baker, the juvenile detention home just outside Buffalo. She still calls my folks Mom and Dad.

SIMMS The first day of training camp, I couldn't believe how fast everybody was. Everybody. Even the big guys. The first two passes I threw were both intercepted—by linebackers. The first one, I let it go, and I said to myself, "That's a nice pass," and a linebacker intercepted it. Then I threw another nice pass, and another linebacker intercepted it. Nobody was that big and that fast in the Ohio Valley Conference. I couldn't do anything right the rest of the day. I wondered what I was doing there.

CONKS The day I graduated from the United States Naval Academy, I became an ensign in the U.S. Navy, an officer and a gentleman. My mother and father attended the ceremony, and they were as proud of me as I was of them.

I was always proud of them. When I went to Canisius High School, most of the kids came from families that had much more money than mine. A lot of them had fathers who were doctors and lawyers. But none of them had a mother and father who were better parents than mine.

My mother got her bachelor's degree after I got mine. Then she got her master's in child development and mental retardation. She's working on her doctorate now. She's fifty, going on nineteen.

SIMMS For two weeks, I didn't do anything. I didn't do anything *right,* anyway. I knew George Young and Ray Perkins had to be sitting around saying, "Oh, my God, what have we done?" I was so bad, it was unbelievable. I was struggling.

It was no fun being a number-one draft choice, knowing everybody was looking at you, wondering about you, especially being a quarterback and from a school nobody had ever heard of.

Gordon King knew what I was going through. He'd been the number-one draft choice in 1978, and even though he was a tackle and he came from Stanford, he was glad to get that off his back. Gordon wasn't very talkative, but one day, after practice, we were in the shower and he said, "I'm glad you're here. I don't envy you."

You get special attention when you're number one. I had to get up in the dining hall each night and sing the Morehead State fight song.

The good thing was that nobody knew the Morehead song. The bad thing was I didn't either. I knew the tune, so I just made up the words. Even Gary Shirk, our tight end, didn't know I was making up the words, and he was the only other guy in the NFL who went to Morehead State.

CONKS Kit McCulley and I stayed at the Naval Academy for several months after graduation, waiting to get into flight school. He taught sailing, and I taught phys. ed. and helped coach the football team. We shared an apartment just outside the gate to the academy. We didn't have to climb over the wall anymore to meet women.

SIMMS I lived in Lyndhurst, New Jersey, my rookie season, just a few miles from Giants Stadium, sharing a house with Brad Benson, an offensive lineman who was my age, but had been with the team for a couple of years.

Brad came out of Penn State in 1977 and was drafted by the New England Patriots. After they cut him, he went home to Altoona, Pennsylvania. He was teaching math in the sixth grade when the principal barged into the classroom and said, "The Giants are on the phone. They want you to go to New York." The kids cheered, and Brad signed with the Giants for the last five games of the season.

Lyndhurst was a real blue-collar town, so Benson and I fit in perfectly. Our neighbors couldn't have been nicer. We'd go off on a road trip, and when we'd come back, the lady next door would've cleaned our house, done our laundry and straightened out our groceries. You could eat off the floor the place was so clean. My clothes were all neatly folded. We were spoiled.

By the end of the season, everybody in Lyndhurst knew there were a couple of Giants living there, and we had visitors all the time.

The veterans were very nice to me. For instance, Brian Kelley, a veteran linebacker, took the time and trouble to teach me how to play gin rummy. Brian wore my ass out for about two years while I learned.

I met Diana in a restaurant not far from Giants Stadium after a game early in my rookie season. I was with a bunch of the guys, and she was with a group of girls, and we all exchanged telephone numbers. I noticed her right away—she was tall and blond—but I was too shy to say anything to her. She and her friends left the place around midnight. I wasn't too shy to call her at 1:00 A.M. and tell her I was sorry I didn't get much of a chance to talk to her.

After we lost our first five games in 1979, Ray Perkins decided he couldn't do any worse with me at quarterback, so he announced that I would start the next game, against Tampa Bay in Giants Stadium. The Bucs had won their first five games, they were the only undefeated team in the NFL and they had Lee Roy Selmon, who was awesome, playing defensive end. I didn't know enough to be scared. Perkins did.

He watched films with me every day. He took me to his house for dinner every night. He was afraid to let me out of his sight. I'd only played in one game, the fifth game, against New Orleans, and even though I had thrown my first NFL touchdown pass, I'd also thrown an interception and messed up a handoff that probably cost us the game. Perkins kept telling me and the press that I had to cut down my mistakes.

I didn't make any against Tampa Bay. I didn't take any chances, either. I only threw about a dozen times, mostly short and safe, and none of them went for touchdowns and none of them was intercepted, either. We won the game. We upset Tampa Bay. The fans at Giants Stadium actually cheered me.

Diana and I had our first date at an automobile agency. I was making an appearance at the agency, and she lived close by. She met me there and, after I signed a few autographs, we went to dinner. I saw her a couple of times during the week leading up to the Tampa Bay game. She lived near Coach Perkins, and after I watched films with him and had dinner at his house, I went over to her house. I'd rather have had dinner with Diana.

CONKS I flew up to Buffalo one weekend and went to see the Bills play, and while I sat in the stands and watched the teams warm up, I made believe there was a new NFL rule that every team had to pick one guy out of the crowd and put him in their starting lineup. I fantasized that the Bills picked me and that they didn't lose much with me in the game. I saw myself racing down the field, diving, stretching, making the catch.

I thought it was a terrific new rule.

Then I went back to Annapolis.

SIMMS Against San Francisco, the week after the Tampa Bay game, I ran for one touchdown and I threw for 300 yards and two touchdowns, both to a rookie wide receiver named Earnest Gray, and we won again in Giants Stadium.

Then we went on the road and won our next two games, in Kansas City and in Los Angeles, and all of a sudden I was undefeated in four games as a starting quarterback in the NFL, and I really didn't know what the hell was going on. All I did was just play.

We played Dallas next. The Cowboys had beaten the Giants nine times in a row. The Cowboys had played in the previous two Super Bowls. But I threw two touchdown passes, and we were beating Dallas, 14–13, until Rafael Septien kicked a field goal for them with three seconds to play. We came that close to winning five in a row.

We wound up with six victories and ten defeats—six and five with me as the starting quarterback—and I made the All-Rookie team.

Diana got used to me calling her and saying, "Well, I'd really like to see you tonight, but I've got to study films." She said she understood that football was my first priority, my first commitment. She really did understand. She still does.

We got married about four months after we met.

1980

In which Simms goes to
Pasadena, and McConkey
goes to Pensacola

SIMMS I went to the Super Bowl after my rookie season. Not
to play in it. To watch it. The NFL brought me and a few
other players out to Los Angeles to talk at some Super Bowl
functions. I picked Pittsburgh to beat the Rams, which wasn't
very hard. We beat the Rams in Los Angeles that year—we
only won one other road game the whole year—and I threw
two touchdown passes against them. If I could do that, imagine what Terry Bradshaw could do.

Terry threw two touchdown passes, too, and I sat in the
stands at the Rose Bowl and watched him team up with John
Stallworth on a 73-yard play that put the Steelers ahead for
good in the fourth quarter. For the second year in a row,
Bradshaw was named the Most Valuable Player in the Super
Bowl. He was a hero to me, with his blond hair, his strong
arm and his lack of an accent.

I wasn't jealous, but I thought I'd sure like to play in a
Super Bowl some day. Especially in the Rose Bowl.

CONKS I started flight school in Pensacola, Florida, early in 1980, and by the time I finished a year later, I had two hundred hours of training in a T-34 Bravo, a fixed-wing turbo-prop, and one hundred hours of training in helicopters, the H-1 Huey and the TH-57 Jet Ranger.

I loved the challenge of flying, and the excitement, but I did have one problem. Once in a while, usually when we were doing aerobatics in the T-34, loops and whirls, I got airsick. So did a lot of other guys. Still it wasn't nearly as bad as the seasickness I suffered when I went on cruises as a midshipman.

Kit McCulley started flight school three months ahead of me, and we shared a townhouse in Pensacola. He always said he singlehandedly got me through flight school. He did help.

SIMMS Diana and I were sitting at home one Sunday morning, not long after we got married, relaxing, watching TV, eating breakfast, and the phone rang. I picked it up and the most urgent voice I'd ever heard said, "Is Phil there?"

"This is Phil," I said.

"This is David Fishof."

"Oh, hi, David," I said. "How ya doing?" I didn't have the slightest idea who he was.

"I'm an agent in New York," Fishof said, "and Drew Pearson was supposed to do an engagement for me up in Albany today, and he can't make it, he canceled on me, and I got to have somebody to fill in, will you do it?" He never took a breath.

"No thanks," I said. "I'm home relaxing with my wife."

"The fee's a thousand dollars," David said.

At the time, the going rate for an appearance by a rookie quarterback from Morehead State was five hundred dollars. A thousand sounded pretty good. I guess David could tell I was tempted.

"Here's what you do," David said. "You got to go to Newark Airport, you got to hurry, you got a plane ticket waiting for you, you can catch it, you can do it.''

"No, I can't," I said. "I just don't want to leave my wife and I appreciate your calling and it's been nice talking to you, David." And I hung up.

He called right back. "I'll get you fifteen hundred," he said. "I won't even take a commission, I'm desperate, those people'll be so disappointed, you got to do it, just show up, please."

I gave in. "Okay," I said, "I'll go."

I went to the airport, picked up the ticket, caught the plane and made the appearance. As soon as I got home, the phone rang. David wanted to know how it went. I told him it went real well, and I appreciated him calling, and he said he was very grateful to me for going. He'd calmed down. He was talking almost slow enough for me to understand him.

I was looking for an agent. I'd had a bad experience with my original agent. An expensive experience. I asked David who he represented, and he said, "Why don't you come in and see me?"

"Yeah," I said, "I think I'll do that."

I went in and met him and liked him right away. The thing I liked best was that he didn't look like an agent. Every agent I'd met when I was coming out of college was the kind you read about, slick, fancy, gold chains, "Yeah, baby, I'll get you this, I'll get you that, trust me, baby."

There was nothing slick or flashy about David. I trusted him right away.

I was one of David's first Giants, and now he represents me and McConkey and Jim Burt and Billy Ard and Brad Benson. He also represents Lou Piniella, the manager of the Yankees, and Vince Ferragamo, who used to play quarterback for the Rams and a few other teams, and most of us have given David autographed pictures as tokens of our appreciation. Every inscription is the same—a vicious and obscene attack upon

David, insulting his intelligence, his character and his scruples.

David keeps all the inscribed pictures framed on the wall over his desk.

CONKS In flight school, we were taught how to survive in the water, which is, obviously, a necessary skill for naval aviators. We learned drown-proofing techniques, relaxing, letting your body go limp. I never could swim fast—I couldn't beat my grandmother in a race—but I learned to stay afloat for a long time. We learned to swim in water with oil burning on the surface: Come straight up perpendicular to the surface, hands first, splashing to clear a path for your head, raise your head, take a breath, submerge, swim several yards, then come straight up again and repeat the procedure.

The worst thing was the helo dunker, a simulated helicopter crash at sea. You got into the shell of a helicopter and then they lowered you into a big pool, and the first couple of times, you weren't blindfolded, and they turned the shell around a few times, and you had to unstrap yourself and swim out from different positions. It wasn't too hard. The door was next to you. You had a frame of reference.

But then they blindfolded you and turned the shell upside down and spun it around, and you had to escape in the darkness, underwater. At the beginning, you kept swimming into walls, and even though you knew you were in a pool, and knew there were divers nearby, it was pretty scary. You were always close to the edge of panic.

Flight training was intense, but it wasn't as tough as getting through the Naval Academy. The academics weren't nearly as difficult, and at the end of the day, you always got to go home.

SIMMS After Diana and I had been married about six months, I came home one day and found a note on the kitchen table that said, "Dear Tom, please put the potatoes in the oven. Love, Diana." When she got home, I said, "Who's Tom?"

"What do you mean, who's Tom?" she said.

"You left a note to Tom to put the potatoes in the oven," I said.

I showed her the note and she started to laugh. "Tom's an old boyfriend of mine," she said. "That's the funniest thing in the world that I wrote down his name instead of yours."

I didn't think it was.

"Did you put the potatoes in the oven?" she said.

"Hell, no," I said. "You told Tom to do that."

CONKS I watched the highlights of the first week of the 1980 NFL season, and I saw Phil Simms throw five touchdown passes against the St. Louis Cardinals, four of them to Earnest Gray. The Giants won the game, 41–35. I liked the way Simms carried himself on the field, brash and cocky, my kind of guy. He looked like he was in charge.

SIMMS I played pretty good against St. Louis. The only Giant quarterback who'd ever thrown more than five touchdown passes in a game was Y. A. Tittle, and he was in the Hall of Fame.

I figured I was on my way there after that first game. Then I threw only four touchdown passes in the next eight games, and we lost all eight, and I figured I was on my way back to Kentucky.

Then I had two more pretty good games. I passed for more than 300 yards against Dallas and for more than 300 yards against Green Bay, and we won both games. The last Giant quarterback to pass for more than 300 yards two games in a row was Y. A. Tittle.

I'd just as soon forget the rest of the season. San Francisco sacked me ten times, and then St. Louis sacked me four, and on one hit against the Cardinals, I banged up my collarbone —and I missed the last three games.

I probably could've played the final game, against the Oakland Raiders, who went on to win the Super Bowl, but there didn't seem to be a whole lot of sense to it. The Raiders beat us, naturally, and we finished the season with four victories and twelve defeats.

The writers reminded us that made seventeen straight seasons for the Giants without going to the playoffs. I was already getting tired of hearing about Tittle, Gifford and Huff.

1981

In which McConkey gets his
wings, and Simms gets hit so
hard he'll never forget it

CONKS In January 1981, in a graduation ceremony in Pensacola, I got my wings of gold. I became, officially, a naval
aviator, which meant that my commitment to serve on active
duty in the U.S. Navy was automatically extended to January
1986, five years from the day I received my wings.

■ Twenty-six of the twenty-eight teams in the National Football League indicated that if they had the first choice in the
1981 college football draft, they would select, from the University of North Carolina, the linebacker Lawrence Taylor.

Two teams indicated they would choose the Heisman Trophy winner, from the University of South Carolina, the running back George Rogers.

The New Orleans Saints were one of the two teams that
preferred Rogers, and fortunately for the New York Giants,
the Saints were the only team in the NFL that had a poorer
record than the Giants in 1980.

The Saints, with the first choice in the draft, picked Rogers. The Giants, with the second, picked Taylor.

Coincidentally, the Giants had just hired as defensive co-ordinator Bill Parcells, an ex-linebacker who loved his fellow linebackers so much he was going to change the Giants defense from a "four-three," four linemen and three linebackers, to a "three-four," three linemen and four linebackers.

Ray Perkins and Bill Parcells named Taylor the fourth starting linebacker. L.T. was All-Pro in his rookie season, and All-Pro every season since. He was not only good. He was frightening.

SIMMS We played New Orleans the third game of the 1981 season, and I couldn't help but think about their quarterback, Archie Manning, and what he'd gone through in his professional career. He had to be one of the greatest college quarterbacks, but he was in his eleventh year with the Saints, and he'd never had a winning season. Manning wound up playing quarterback for fifteen years in the NFL without a single winning season. My first couple of years in New York, I wondered sometimes if I'd ever play on a winning team.

We had a winning record, two and one, after we beat the Saints, 20–7. I played pretty good, my only 300-yard game of the season. It was a real good day for Morehead State. Gary Shirk, our tight end, caught eleven of my passes, which tied the team record for receptions in a game. We were still the only two Morehead State players in the NFL.

We had three straight victories and a five-three record going into our game against the New York Jets. They whipped us, 26–7, and their defensive line—Joe Klecko and Marty Lyons and Mark Gastineau and Abdul Salaam, the Sack Exchange, they called them—sacked me nine times. But the sacks weren't the worst part of it. Not even close.

I took the absolute worst beating of my life on one pass

play. Gastineau was playing to my right, and he must have stunted, circled behind the other linemen, and then come straight up the middle. I dropped back and all I could see was Gastineau, coming right at me. And wouldn't you know it? Who came open but the tight end over the middle?

So I had to stand there and get up on my tiptoes and stick my arm up as high as I could and then throw the ball. And when I did, Gastineau hit me right in the middle of my chest and—no exaggeration—drove me five, six, seven yards in the air, and then I slammed into the ground, back first. It hurt so much I almost lost control of my bodily functions.

I looked up and Gastineau was leaning over me and I knew what he was thinking. He was thinking, *I've killed him*. I still don't know how I got up and walked off the field.

I never forgot that hit. I never will.

Later in the same game, Gastineau chased me out of bounds and hit me very gently by his standards, and as I fell, I slipped and suffered a pulled groin muscle that kept me out of our next game.

CONKS I followed Kit again, into specialized training in helicopters, specifically in the CH-46, the Sea Knight, a cargo helicopter that was also capable of carrying as many as twenty people. The marines used the Sea Knight to transport troops in Vietnam.

With its tandem rotors, the CH-46 was very good for "vertrep," vertical replenishment of supplies. We carried loads externally and dropped them onto ships. It was quicker and safer than one ship going alongside another to deliver supplies.

Strangely, I never got airsick in helicopters.

SIMMS The end of the 1981 season was really exciting. We had to win four of our last five games to get into the playoffs. We had to beat Dallas, Los Angeles and Philadelphia, all of whom had been in the playoffs the previous year. We had to come from behind in all three of those games. We did it, and I had nothing to do with it.

I missed the last five games of the regular season, sidelined by a separated right shoulder, separated when Dave Butz of the Washington Redskins sacked me late in our eleventh game. Scott Brunner, who was just in his second season, took my place.

With nine victories and seven defeats, the Giants went to the playoffs for the first time in eighteen years, and I watched Scott throw three touchdown passes to beat the Philadelphia Eagles, who'd gone to the Super Bowl the previous season, in the NFC wild-card game.

1982

In which McConkey finds that
ships make him sick, and Simms
finds that Jets make him hurt

SIMMS Scott Brunner threw three more touchdown passes against San Francisco in the National Conference semifinals, but it wasn't quite enough. The 49ers beat us, 38–24, then went on to win the Super Bowl. Joe Montana, the quarterback Bill Walsh drafted after the Giants took me, was named the Most Valuable Player in Super Bowl XVI.

I went to the Super Bowl for the second time—to make an appearance for HBO. I hated watching the game. I told David Fishof not to arrange any more appearances for me at Super Bowls. I didn't want to go again unless I was playing in it.

CONKS They tortured me physically and mentally, blew smoke and breathed onions into my face, smacked me against a wall, forced me to lie down in a coffin, even tried to tempt me with a beautiful woman. They wanted me to sign a confession that I was a war criminal. They urged me to denounce my own country and embrace communism.

51

They were my teachers—my captors and "counselors"—in the prisoner-of-war "reeducation" camp that I had to attend before I could be sent overseas to fly.

The navy operates two simulated POW camps, one in San Diego and one in Maine. After I finished my helicopter training, I was sent, in the dead of winter, to the camp in Maine. To start my ordeal, my test, they set me loose on the side of a freezing mountain.

I wore snowshoes to keep from disappearing into the drifts, and I carried two sleeping bags so that at night, if I found a decent shelter, I could slip inside the two sleeping bags, strip off my wet clothes, and put them between the two bags to dry.

The idea was to avoid capture for as long as possible. I lasted one day.

They caught me when I wandered too close to a road, slapped me around, took me to a small shanty, and in Russian accents ordered me to take off all my clothes, from parka and boots to thermal underwear. They threw my clothes into a huge pile of prisoners' clothing. Then, after a doctor examined me, they kicked my ass, told me to grab a set of clothes from the pile, any set, quickly, and put the clothes on and get moving. I was lucky. The pair of pants I picked stayed up without me holding them.

They did everything to demean you, to degrade you. They put you in a small solitary cell and when a guard barked, "Assume the posish," you had to squat with your elbows on your thighs and your palms facing up. If you wanted to pee, you had to say, "War criminal number so-and-so requests permission to urinate," and then they gave you a rusted coffee can. They pretended to offer fruit to prisoners on your right and left, but there was no fruit, it was only a frustrating ruse. They played monotonous martial music over and over. They bombarded you with speeches about how great communism is, and how democracy sucks.

You lost track of day and night, and, disoriented, you wanted desperately to sleep. You could sleep. You could rest. You could have food. All you had to do was sign the confession. A few prisoners did—and washed out. They couldn't go overseas, not to fly, not to risk capture behind enemy lines. You knew it was only an exercise, but they played so many games with your mind and body, you almost believed it was real. You didn't know when it was going to end.

If you held out long enough, two or three days, as most of us did, you suddenly heard rifle shots and machine-gun fire and grenades exploding, and a rescue force swept into the POW camp and routed the "Russians" and unfurled an American flag, and then you heard the strains of "The Star-Spangled Banner," and, I'll tell you, there wasn't a dry eye in the place.

After that, training camp was easy.

I spent five months in the Mediterranean, visiting exotic ports, Haifa and Tunis and Majorca, and flying helicopters, assigned to a store ship, delivering supplies to other ships. Landing on a cruiser was a real challenge, especially at night, on rough seas, making a descending, decelerating turn into a tight landing zone, barely ten to fifteen feet between rotors and superstructure, your depth perception destroyed by the darkness. You never knew when your survival training was going to come in handy.

I liked flying, but I hated being on a ship at sea. I got seasick every day. I liked taking my helicopter up just to escape from the rolling ship.

Ever since I was an underclassman at Annapolis, I'd been getting seasick, but everybody told me not to worry about it, I'd adjust, I'd get over it. I never did. I suspect there may be a correlation between motion sickness and athletic balance, that the canals in my inner ear may be too sensitive, too attuned to shifts in equilibrium. I have no proof of this, but

I've met other athletes with wonderful balance who've also suffered from motion sickness.

In July, the navy cut short my Mediterranean tour and shipped me back to Norfolk, where doctors began sticking needles in me, trying to figure out why I got seasick and how they could cure me. I was a guinea pig for all their theories.

I wanted to stay in the navy. I looked into supply, into intelligence, into all phases of naval operations. But the bottom line was: If I couldn't go to sea, I couldn't be competitive as an officer.

My navy career was obviously in jeopardy.

SIMMS Scott Brunner got us off to a 10–0 lead at halftime against Pittsburgh in our second exhibition game. Then I took over. I threw three interceptions and took three sacks, and by the time we lost the game, I think everybody in Giants Stadium had booed me except Diana. I'm not sure about Diana.

Afterward, a reporter asked me what I thought of the fans' reaction. The question wasn't a good one. The answer wasn't either. "I really don't care what the fans think," I said, among other things. "They don't understand what's going on. I don't play for them."

The remarks were made out of frustration and were taken out of context—they probably wouldn't have sounded too good in context either—and the newspaper ran a headline that said: SIMMS: I DON'T CARE ABOUT FANS.

I received a lot of mail in the next few days indicating that I was about as popular in New Jersey as the Ayatollah Khomeini.

CONKS Lesley was the most beautiful girl I'd ever met. The first time I saw her, I was having dinner in Virginia Beach with six other girls. Lesley was our waitress. She had light brown hair and terrific legs. She was wearing a mini-skirt and cowboy boots. I couldn't stop staring.

While Phil McConkey was diving for passes at the United States Naval Academy in the late 1970s, Phil Simms was displaying professional passing form at Morehead State.

Even when they were both baseball players, Whitey Simms of Okolona (*top, second row, second from right*) didn't enjoy the spotlight as much as Phil McConkey of Anunciation (*below, with trophy*) did.

Simms plays the role of golfer as well as Conks plays a variety of roles: As a child, as a girl (walking to school with his teenaged girl friend, Connie McQuestion, on Halloween) and as a midshipman at Annapolis.

Running at the Naval Academy (*above, left*) or with the Giants (*above, right*), Conks has always gripped the ball securely in his right hand. At Navy, he was MVP in the Holiday Bowl (*right*) and scored a touchdown against Army (*below*).

When Simms was passing for the Morehead State Eagles, it wasn't an upset for the other team to have more points on the scoreboard.

Simms may team up with McConkey for touchdowns, but in business, his partner is agent David Fishof, who negotiates contracts and commercials.

Clockwise from top:
Jeana McConkey,
Phil's mother, posed
with a range of stars
at the Super Bowl,
from Mark Bavaro
to Tom Cruise to
Diana and Phil
Simms. Conks's
father, Joe, and his
sister, Debbie, also
got into the act.

Phil Simms has always listened to his coaches, from Henderson Wilson at Southern High (*above, left*) to Wayne Chapman at Morehead State (*above, right*) to Ray Perkins (*below*) in his early Giants years to Bill Parcells (*bottom*) in his later Giants years.

Ira Golden

Too often during his first five seasons in a Giants uniform, Simms found himself sitting on the bench, frustrated by injury, wondering whether he would ever get the chance to demonstrate the ability he knew he had.

The other girls noticed that my attention was straying. They got in their shots. They said her skirt was out of style, and so were her boots. They didn't say her body was.

Lesley, I found out, was living with a girl I knew. They didn't have much room. I told Lesley she could live in my townhouse. I also told her I was an officer and a gentleman. At first, she paid rent. She paid next to nothing. Then I reduced the rent.

Lesley was the first girl I'd ever lived with. She was also the only one, so far. She was eighteen. I was twenty-five, and I thought I was getting old, and she made me feel young again. We lived together for four months.

SIMMS For me, the 1982 season ended before it officially began. It ended in the first quarter of our third exhibition game. It ended when Abdul Salaam of the Jets hit me low and Joe Klecko hit me high.

I was rushing to get a pass off, and all my weight was still on my back foot, my right foot, and my right leg was extended. When Salaam and Klecko hit me, my right knee turned to jelly. I felt sick to my stomach. I tried to stand up, but I couldn't. I knew immediately the season was over. I had torn ligaments in my knee.

I was helped off the field and, for a change, nobody booed.

I hate playing against the Jets, especially in exhibition games. Because of the rivalry created by the media and by the fans, the games always have a special intensity. They're always a little more physical than they have to be. The quarterbacks always get killed. I'd rather face the Bears or the Broncos any day.

They operated on my knee, and when I went home, after a week in the hospital, I couldn't sleep. I'd get up in the middle of the night and walk around the house. I hated not being able to play. I couldn't even watch the games. I'd turn on the television and then I'd walk out of the room.

CONKS All fall, I kept hearing that since the navy couldn't cure my seasickness, they were going to let me go. When I went home for Christmas, I told my folks that I might have to start looking for a job. "Why don't you try football?" my father said.

I thought he was crazy. I hadn't played a football game in four years. But my mother and Kit McCulley both thought my father was right, I should try football, and the more they talked about it, the more I liked it.

I didn't want to go through life wondering if I could have made it. I didn't want to be forty-five, sitting in front of the TV set, thinking, "What if . . . ?"

The old fire was rekindled. I started dreaming about Super Bowl touchdowns again.

SIMMS At least I didn't miss a full season. But that was only because we didn't have a full season in 1982. The players' strike shortened the season to nine games. Scott Brunner was the starting quarterback in all nine games. We won four and lost five and just missed getting into the playoffs.

SWEAT
1983–1985

■ Of the fifty-two players who were New York Giants in Pasadena on January 25, 1987—forty-five active and seven on injured reserve—only twelve had joined the team before 1983. Of course, there were eight starters among those twelve—including the Big Three of Morris, Simms and Taylor, and the Old Three of Benson, Carson and Martin—but most of the team had not put on Giant uniforms until after Ray Perkins left.

Perkins resigned at the end of 1982 to return to his alma mater, the University of Alabama, to succeed a legend, Bear Bryant, as the head coach of the Crimson Tide. Perkins, a stern, stiff man who seemed to be gritting his teeth all the time, had shown the Giants that they could win, that they could reach the playoffs. He had also shown them that they could work very hard and still survive.

To succeed Perkins, George Young chose the team's defensive coordinator, Bill Parcells, born and raised in New Jersey only minutes away from the Meadowlands swamp that later became the site of Giants Stadium, a Giants fan all his life. When Parcells was in high school and in college, the Giants were the most successful team in football, the most glamorous.

"I think life's too short to walk around with your teeth gritted all the time," Parcells said, when he succeeded Perkins. "I like to joke. I like to laugh." The defensive players knew that he also liked to yell. "Our players know me," he said. "You can usually tell what I'm thinking by the expression on my face."

Parcells was, and is, like the players he most cherishes, a gym rat, a sports junkie. He was a basketball and football star in high school, then a linebacker at Wichita State College in Kansas. He started his coaching career at Hastings College in Nebraska. At Hastings, he lined the field before practice and washed the uniforms after practice. He paid his dues.

He was an assistant at Hastings, Wichita State, West Point, Florida State, Vanderbilt and Texas Tech before he became head coach at the Air Force Academy. He started his professional career coaching linebackers for the New England Patriots in 1980, then the following year joined the Giants. He still wasn't quite forty.

Parcells retained five assistant coaches who had been hired by Perkins—Bill Belichick, now the defensive coordinator; Romeo Crennel, the special teams coach; Ron Erhardt, the offensive coordinator; Pat Hodgson, the receivers coach; and Lamar Leachman, the defensive line coach. Ironically, Erhardt, as the head coach of the Patriots, had hired Parcells in 1980 to coach his linebackers. Neither of the top two assistants—Belichick, from Wesleyan University, and Erhardt, from Jamestown College in North Dakota—had ever played professional football. Parcells hadn't either.

In 1983, George Young and Parcells and their assistants and scouts began filling in the holes in the Giants lineup. They struck gold. They chose Terry Kinard from Clemson in the first round of the draft, and Kinard became a starting safety as a rookie. They chose Leonard Marshall from Louisiana State in the second round, and Marshall became a starting defensive end as a rookie. They chose Karl Nelson from Iowa State in the third round, and Nelson, after missing the entire 1983 season because of an injury, became a starting offensive tackle as a rookie. They chose Perry Williams from North Carolina State in the seventh round, and Williams, who also spent 1983 on injured reserve, became a starting cornerback as a 1984 rookie.

The Giants signed Zeke Mowatt from Florida State as a free agent, and Mowatt became the starting tight end as a rookie. They drafted two linebackers, Robbie Jones and Andy Headen, who played in Super Bowl XXI.

In addition, the Giants agreed to take a look at a free agent from the United States Naval Academy named Phil Mc-Conkey.

1983

In which McConkey faces the dismal prospect of going to Guantanamo Bay, and Simms faces the even more dismal prospect of going to Tampa Bay

SIMMS I was sorry to see Ray Perkins go, and I was glad. I appreciated what he'd done for me, the faith he'd shown drafting me in the first round, and I appreciated what he'd done for the team, too. He stepped into a country-club situation, a situation that had to be straightened out, and he was the right person to straighten it out. He was tough. He ran the show. He changed attitudes. He was great at spotting weaknesses.

But he wasn't as good at spotting strengths. He wasn't as good at giving encouragement, building your confidence, making you feel secure. That wasn't his style. He was better at kicking you in the butt than patting you on the back. I needed some stroking.

Still Perkins made the Giants a better team in his four years, no question about that. The first couple of years, I'd gone into too many games knowing we couldn't win. But by 1983, I figured that with another good draft and another year of experience, we could be as good as anybody.

I liked the idea of playing for Bill Parcells. I always knew he'd be a head coach. He talked like a head coach. He didn't undermine Perkins or anything like that, he was just always trying to learn everything he could about offense as well as defense. We used to sit around and talk, and he'd tell me about the kind of quarterback he wanted to have—strong, tough, bold, confident, capable of throwing long—and I'd go home and tell Diana, "He's talking about me,"

I was really looking forward to the 1983 season. My knee was healing perfectly, and I felt that mentally and physically I was finally ready to play quarterback in the National Football League.

CONKS In January and February, between shore duty and more medical tests, I worked out in Norfolk, sometimes in the snow, trying to get myself in shape to try out for pro football.

I really didn't know how to get ready. George Welsh, my coach at Navy, told me to work on my speed. At Navy, I'd run the forty in four-point-five seconds sometimes, but logically I figured I must have lost a step or two in four years. George told me that, to be considered by the pros, I couldn't run the forty any slower than four-point-six seconds.

I started running forties on my lunch hour at Norfolk. I ran approximately forty yards—I had no way of measuring it exactly—about forty times each lunch hour. I ran ten forties as fast as I could with maybe fifteen seconds between them, then rested for about five minutes, then ran another set of ten as fast as I could. I usually ran four sets in less than an hour, a total of 1,600 yards. In other words, I *sprinted* almost a mile on my lunch hour. I pushed myself to the point of exhaustion, and sometimes beyond. I was afraid to do anything less.

It wasn't smart. It wasn't scientific. I should've varied my schedule, run twenties some days, hundreds other days, built up my speed and my stamina. But I didn't know any better.

Then, after my duty day was over, I went to the gym and lifted for a couple of hours. I lifted as much weight as I could for as many repetitions as I could. I didn't know what I was doing there, either. I was just a buzz saw, going wild, trying to stretch my physical limits.

Two of my assistant coaches at Navy, Tom Bresnahan and Len Fontes, joined the New York Giants as assistants under Bill Parcells, and another, Steve Belichick, had a son, Bill, who was already on the Giants staff. While I worked on my body, they worked on getting me a tryout with the Giants.

Late in February, just before my twenty-sixth birthday, I took a week's leave and went down to Pensacola to visit Kit. I was dying to know my time in the forty. We took a fold-out wooden ruler, four feet long, and we measured out forty yards on the street, marking each yard with black spray paint. The marks were still on the street in Pensacola, faint but visible, when I was playing for the Giants in the Super Bowl.

I warmed up, stretched my muscles, then moved to the start of the 40-yard course. Then I took off. Kit knew how to time me; he knew to use the forefinger, because it's quicker, not the thumb, to click the stopwatch. When I hit the finish line, Kit looked at his watch and said, "Whew!"

I trotted back to him, and he didn't say anything. He just held up the watch—a digital stopwatch—and I read it: Four-point-four-eight! I was ecstatic. I ran two more forties, and Kit caught one in four-point-five-three and the other in four-point-four-nine. I knew then I had a legitimate chance to make the NFL.

Kit and I went out to celebrate that night and, by our standards, we drank a lot. We both drink like women, and we drink the stuff women drink. We had margaritas, and we talked about my going to New York, being an underdog and a Naval Academy graduate, doing something that no one had ever done, except Roger Staubach, doing it in the media capital of the world, playing in a Super Bowl, reaping the rewards of endorsements, speeches, a book, dozens of fantasies that, eventually, became realities.

Then I returned to Norfolk, still grounded and landlocked, and while I waited to be released from the navy, some of my fellow officers heard about my dream of playing in the NFL, and they laughed at the dream and at me. They figured I had a better chance of becoming an admiral than a pro football player. They said there was no way I could do it. There was no way I was going to give them the satisfaction of being right.

SIMMS I probably didn't work as hard as McConkey did getting ready for the 1983 season—I'm serious about it; I'm not crazy—but I worked hard. I spent a lot of time on the machines building up my knee. I knew I was going to be faster on my feet than I'd ever been before. Or at least I wasn't going to be as slow. I'd never exactly been known for my swiftness.

I just wanted to have one healthy season. It was funny, but when I got drafted, I never thought I'd get hurt. I wasn't fragile. I was big and strong. I'd never been hurt in college. That was one of the things the NFL teams liked about me. I looked like I could stand up under the punishment.

Before we even started working out, Coach Parcells told the press that the quarterback job was wide open, that it didn't belong to me or to Scott Brunner or to anybody. I figured it was wide open all right, wide open for me to take it over again.

CONKS Right after the college draft, the Giants invited me to their rookie mini-camp in April.

I could hardly wait. I'd been transferred from Norfolk to the Naval Academy, to work in the physical education department. I heard rumors that my discharge papers were being typed. I knew I'd dazzle the Giants in the mini-camp.

Just before I went to camp, I saw the movie *Flashdance*

and I identified with Jennifer Beals, the girl who played the lead role. She burned to make it as a dancer, and I knew exactly how she felt.

I wouldn't mind going out with her, either.

SIMMS I didn't think he'd make it.

Of course, I noticed him right away at the mini-camp. In the first place, he was the only white wide receiver among the rookies, and in the second, he dove for every ball he couldn't catch any other way. I never saw anyone make so many diving catches. I remember one where he sprinted down the sideline, flat out, dove and made a great catch, and when he came up, both his elbows were blood-red. "Hey, leave a little bark on," Pat Hodgson, the receivers coach, yelled to him.

I could tell right away that McConkey was serious about trying out for the Giants.

But I wasn't all that impressed, because you see guys like that in every mini-camp. He reminded me of another kid we had from Navy a couple of years earlier, a strong safety with a world of guts, but just not quite enough size or speed. I put McConkey in the same category. I figured he was probably a very tough kid with a great work ethic, but he wasn't going to be a professional football player, at least not in the National Football League.

I just had one conversation with him at mini-camp. From all his diving, he had rug burns that were unbelievable. "Man, you better be careful," I said. "Those things are gonna kill you. Those rug burns are worse than getting injured sometimes."

"Yeah," he said. "I got to pad up."

The third day of the camp, the final day, he had pads all over him.

CONKS The morning of the final day of the rookie mini-camp, the Giants offered me a contract. They offered me $45,000 for

1983 if I made the team, $5,000 above the NFL minimum, plus a signing bonus of $3,500.

I hesitated only because Norm Pollom of the Buffalo Bills, who had scouted me in college, had asked me to check with him before I signed with the Giants.

As we were loosening up before the final afternoon workout, Parcells walked up to me and asked me why I hadn't signed. "Was it the money?" he said.

Before I could answer, he said, "I'll throw in another thousand. I'll make it forty-five hundred for signing."

"I'll take it," I said, before he could change his mind.

"Should I type it?" Parcells said.

"Go ahead."

I signed and began dreaming of making Super Bowl catches for the New York Giants, not the Buffalo Bills.

SIMMS It didn't take McConkey long to start getting his name in the papers. The *Newark Star-Ledger* said he caught ten passes in one practice that were uncatchable. They said he was the outstanding rookie in mini-camp.

CONKS The morning after the last day of the mini-camp, I woke up early because the wall in my hotel room was shaking. It didn't take me long to figure out what was happening. The rookie in the next room had a girl in with him. I was amazed. How could he even think of that when he was trying out for the National Football League?

When I returned to Annapolis, I found that my discharge still hadn't come through. I called Capt. Jack Fellows in the medical section at the Department of the Navy. Captain Fellows had spent six and a half years as a prisoner of war in Vietnam, then had served at Annapolis as the liaison between the football team and the administration. I'd gotten to know him at the Academy. He knew my medical history and had recommended that I be discharged.

Captain Fellows told me that my discharge had proceeded routinely until it reached the desk of a Commodore Ustick, who had to give final approval. Someone apparently had alerted Commodore Ustick to the fact that I was hoping to become a professional football player. He was holding up my papers.

I called the commodore's office and made an appointment to see him. I went to his office and, at his request, reviewed my situation with him, the history of my seasickness, the unproductive medical tests, the frustration of being a naval officer who could not go to sea.

Commodore Ustick said he was not going to let me out of the navy.

I couldn't believe it. "But, sir," I said, "I'm not competitive in the navy. I don't have a prayer of getting anywhere in the navy, and now I have an opportunity to start another career."

"You have an obligation to the navy," Commodore Ustick said. He, too, had been stationed at the Naval Academy when I was on the football team. But unlike Captain Fellows, Commodore Ustick had no sympathy for the midshipmen who made the sacrifices that were necessary to combine athletics and academics. People who knew him told me he hated athletes.

I started to cry. My dream of a naval career had been shattered, and he was shattering my dream of a football career. The tears poured out of me, and Commodore Ustick, who seemed to be enjoying my discomfort, said that not only was I staying in, but that he was going to recommend that I be sent to Guantanamo Bay.

He wanted to ship me to the hell hole of the earth, to the base in Cuba every man in the navy dreads, especially every *single* man, to Guantanamo, where social life does not exist.

Commodore Ustick thought it would be nice if I served two or three years at Guantanamo Bay.

I went back to Annapolis and got a lawyer and explained the situation to him, and he felt that between the merits of my case and the influence of his contacts, he could get Commodore Ustick's decision reversed. He said it was a waste of taxpayers' money to keep me in the navy any longer.

The attorney warned me that it wasn't easy to reverse a decision made at flag rank, but he felt reasonably confident we would be able to do it.

I took my accumulated leave time and went off to training camp in July, to the dorms and athletic facilities of Pace College in Pleasantville, New York, hoping that the navy would release me, and that the Giants wouldn't.

I treated my first practice on the first day of training camp as if it were my last. I went full tilt, no holding back, hustling every second. I even sprinted to get a sip of water. "Hey, you got to cool your motor," Pat Hodgson, the assistant coach in charge of the wide receivers, told me. "Calm down. This is a long camp. Save something."

Parcells noticed me, too. "You're going to be here a long time," he said. "I'm going to give you a long look. So just cool down."

I couldn't.

I had that free-agent mentality, that feeling that no matter how hot I was or how tired or how sore, I had to keep pushing myself, driving myself, whipping myself. I had to do more than the guy who had been picked in the draft. I had to work harder than anyone else.

I figured it was the only way I had a chance.

The hardest part of training camp was going to sleep at night. I couldn't do it. I lay in bed and, if I closed my eyes, I lived the whole day over again. Did I run hard enough? Did I hit hard enough? Did I try hard enough? What could I have done differently? What could I have done better? What did I learn? What do I still have to learn? The questions chased each other through my mind.

I got up, walked around, did some exercises, went back to bed and faced the same questions. I tried to imagine myself in a serene setting. I tried to think relaxing thoughts. Nothing worked. I even tried sleeping pills once in a while, and they just made me more alert.

You know how some pills for colds carry a warning that they may make you drowsy? But they also say they may cause excitability in children? Those pills always cause excitability in me. I suppose that tells a lot about me.

I was able to get some sleep about every other night. But it didn't seem to slow me down.

SIMMS "C'mon, McConkey," I said, "let's go have a beer." We had just finished lifting weights together after practice, and I needed some company. None of the other quarterbacks —Scott Brunner, Jeff Rutledge or a kid named Mark Reed— drank at all. Not that I was much of a drinker. But at least I could sit at the bar and cuss and act like I was a drinker. I may not be a good drinker, but I'm a great cusser.

I wasn't in much of a mood, anyway, to socialize with the other quarterbacks. It was nothing personal but the competition among us was getting to me. Parcells kept saying the job was wide open. I knew he had to give the other guys a chance, and I knew I had missed the whole '82 season, and half of '81, but I also knew I deserved the job. I don't brag much, I know when I'm horseshit, but I also know what I can do. I drank more during that training camp than I did at any other.

We went to Foley's, which was a neighborhood bar in Pleasantville, where the older Giants used to hang out. I had a beer in there my rookie year with a veteran defensive end named Jack Gregory, who'd been an All-Pro. "Buddy, you got a lot to look forward to,'' Gregory told me. That was his way of saying goodbye. He left camp the next morning, ended his NFL career.

Now it was my turn to have a beer with a rookie at Foley's. McConkey really nursed his beer. He drinks like a girl, anyway. We sat catty-corner on barstools, and I did all the talking. Every now and then I'd throw him a bone, hoping he'd say something back. But he didn't say much. I thought he was just shy, but when I look back, I guess he was intimidated.

CONKS I thought I was sitting with a god. I'd been a pro football fan all my life, and here I was drinking a beer with the quarterback for the New York Giants. With Phil Simms! He was famous. Even if he hadn't played much the previous two seasons, he was a star to me. And he was being so nice to me.

I asked him about the competition with Brunner and Rutledge, and he said nothing but good things about both of them. But he made it clear he intended to be the starting quarterback.

I tried to keep up with him, drinking, but he had two or three beers, and I just couldn't. I got all my drinking out of my system when I was young. I came from an Italian family and there was always wine around. I've got pictures of me when I was five years old, holding a Genesee beer and a drumstick. I drank a whole quart of beer when I was in junior high. I guess I had my fill then.

I couldn't wait to call Kit to tell him I'd gone out with Phil Simms. I liked Simms from the moment I met him in mini-camp. A lot of guys snub rookies, but Simms always went out of his way to be friendly. He treated a rookie just like he treated a ten-year veteran. He treated a rookie with respect.

He still does.

The uniform, number 93, was too big for me, but I thought it was the greatest outfit I'd ever worn. When I stood in front of the mirror in the locker room, inspecting myself before our first exhibition game, against the New York Jets, I was shaking, I was so nervous. I couldn't believe it. I was a professional football player, at least for one night.

I was on the punt-return team, and another rookie and I were assigned to double-team one of the Jets who was split out to the side. We knocked him down, jumped on top of him, dug our elbows into him, kept him down. We wanted to make sure that when the coaches watched the film, they'd notice that we had done our job.

"Take it easy, you little SOB," the referee shouted at me. "You keep it up, and I'll kick you out."

We beat the Jets, 23–16.

SIMMS And I didn't play. Not one down. Coach Parcells played Jeff Rutledge in the first half and Scott Brunner in the second, and I watched.

I wasn't sure whether Parcells kept me out of the game because he wanted to protect me from Gastineau and Klecko or because he wanted to protect me from the fans in the stands.

"I wanted to create circumstances that would not hurt Phil's chances of performing well," Parcells told a reporter. "It was against the Jets. We were using two young offensive tackles. He was coming off an injury. It was in front of the hometown fans."

All I knew was that my chances of performing well were very slim if I didn't get into the game.

CONKS They came close. They cut my roommate. His name was Cormac Carney, another wide receiver, and he was a freshman at the Air Force Academy when I was a senior at Navy. He left the Academy, transferred to UCLA and made All-Pac Ten for two seasons. He didn't seem too upset at being cut. He wanted to go see his girlfriend in California, anyway.

Even without a roommate, I couldn't sleep. But at least I didn't have to be quiet. The first day I was alone, I turned on the radio at 6:00 A.M., and I got a brand-new station—WHTZ-FM, or Z-100, as they call it—with a familiar disk jockey named Scott Shannon. I used to listen to him when I was at Annapolis and he was in Washington. He was on WPGC— Where People Get Cash. I got through some tough times at the Naval Academy listening to him.

SIMMS Parcells started me in our second exhibition game, against the Steelers, in Pittsburgh, and I played pretty good. I completed ten out of fifteen passes, and two or three others could have been caught. We beat the Steelers, 22–13. Brunner played the second half, and I felt I clearly did a better job. Still, in practice, Parcells kept splitting everything three ways, among Scott, Jeff and me, and I didn't like it. I couldn't get into any rhythm. I didn't say a whole lot, but I wasn't happy.

CONKS I played on the kickoff team against Pittsburgh, and I tried to beat the ball downfield. I almost did. I made two solo tackles inside the 10-yard line.

"Good job you're doing on the kickoffs," Mark Haynes, our All-NFL cornerback, told me after the game. "Keep it up."

I appreciated the compliment. Haynes almost never talked to rookies.

SIMMS I couldn't understand, after all the things Parcells had told me about the kind of quarterback he liked, why he hadn't already picked me. I guess maybe the way I perceived myself wasn't the way I projected myself to him.

CONKS Brunner was cool and collected, on the field and off. In the morning, he'd get up early, drive out to get a copy of *USA Today,* read it at the breakfast table, calm and smooth. At practice, he'd drop back and throw the ball, drop back and throw the ball, just as calm and smooth. Scott was a real nice person.

Simms was nice, too, but he was fiery. If he made a mistake, he'd swear at himself, he'd show his emotions, and, if he did something right, he'd pump his fist. I thought he'd be the quarterback. He was more like me.

A couple of days before we played our final exhibition game, against Miami, I found out for certain that the navy wasn't going to discharge me. I thought about telling Parcells right away, but I decided to wait till after the Miami game. I wanted to play against the Dolphins. They'd played in the Super Bowl that year.

The Dolphins beat us badly, and when Simms came out of the game in the third quarter, after taking a terrible pounding, always hanging in, risking his knee, risking his career, the fans booed him as if it were all his fault. I don't know how he stood it for all those years.

I told Parcells the next morning about the navy. He seemed disappointed. He still had a couple of cuts to make, but I'm pretty sure I would've made the team. I might not have been active at the start of the season, but after Floyd Eddings, a wide receiver, and Leon Bright, the punt returner, got hurt, I think I would've been playing.

Instead, I was put on military reserve, which I don't think had been used since World War II.

I was proud of what I'd accomplished, but I was also bitter and frustrated. I would've been a New York Giant, if I hadn't been cut by Commodore Ustick.

SIMMS Parcells told Brunner and me that he would make his decision the Tuesday morning after the Miami exhibition, the day we began preparing for our opening game against Los Angeles. I went to the stadium Tuesday feeling confident. I knew I didn't do much against Miami, but Scott didn't either, and I believed that, between the exhibition games and the practices, I'd played well enough to get my job back. I knew I was the better quarterback, that's all there was to it.

I saw Scott as I came into the locker room, and he looked at me kind of funny, but I figured that was just because of the situation we were in. I didn't know he'd already been to see Parcells. I didn't know he already knew what was happening.

Then Parcells walked in and said, "Phil, I'd like to see you," and I said, "Okay, good, Coach," and I marched into his office, figuring he was going to tell me I had the job. He sat me down and looked at me and said, very fast, much faster than he usually talks, "Phil you're second string I gave the job to Scott."

I said, "What did you say?"

He repeated it, and I said, "You've got to be kidding."

"No, I'm not kidding," he said. "You don't like it? You can't accept it?"

"You're damned right I don't like it, and there's no way I can accept it," I said.

I was in shock. I was hurt and angry and confused, and I said things it wasn't like me to say. "You can get on the phone right now," I said, "and you can trade my ass because I ain't ever playing for you again. I don't want to have anything to do with this team."

I still can't believe I said those things. I can believe I felt them, but I can't believe I said them.

But I think it was the most upset I've ever been in my life. I mean, Mark Gastineau didn't hit me as hard as Parcells did. Joe Klecko and Abdul Salaam didn't hurt me as much as Parcells did.

He tried to calm me down, to get me to go to a meeting, but I wouldn't listen. "I'm not going to no meeting," I said. It was the low point of my life. I just walked out. There was no excuse for the way I acted, but I think what made me so angry was that I thought the whole thing was a charade, that Parcells had his mind made up all along to go with Brunner, that he had never really given me a chance. He said he gave me a chance. "I gave Phil every opportunity to jump out at me," he told a reporter. But then he added, "I know more about Scott. That's what I'm going with."

I stormed out of the locker room and went to the pay phone and called my agent and said, "David, get me out of here. Get me traded. I don't care where." I told Fishof what had happened, and that I had burned all my bridges, that I could never play in New York again. David got all excited the way he does and said they couldn't get away with this, and any team in the league would be happy to have me, and they really needed a quarterback in Houston and in New Orleans, and don't forget about Donald Trump and his team, the New York Generals, in the rival United States Football League. Trump had already tried to get L.T. away from the Giants. David was going to see what he could do.

In the middle of our conversation, I saw McConkey come out of the locker room, carrying his gear. He was leaving, too.

CONKS I could see Simms wasn't happy—I could hear it, too—but I didn't want to walk past him without saying goodbye. "See ya, Phil," I called, and I started to go out the tunnel, but he yelled, "Hey, wait a minute," and he put the phone down and, despite what he was going through, came over and shook my hand and wished me luck and said he'd see me down the road.

"I'm gonna be back here," I said.

"I'm not," he said.

SIMMS Bill Parcells wanted to trade me.

George Young didn't want to trade me.

Wellington Mara didn't want to trade me.

It was the coach against the general manager and the owner. Guess who wins that fight?

The newspapers were full of stories that I was going to Houston, or to New Orleans, or to Tampa Bay, or to Atlanta, but those stories were all David, all Fishof's doing. He was on the phone to Texas half the time, and to reporters the rest of the time, doing what an agent ought to do, doing everything he could to force the trade I wanted.

It was true that I wanted to be traded. It was true that I thought Houston and New Orleans were up-and-coming teams that could use me. It was true that I told David I was willing to be a backup quarterback anywhere except in New York. It was all true, but it didn't make any difference.

The Giants weren't going to trade me.

The only reason Parcells wanted to get rid of me was that he was afraid I was going to cause trouble. I tried to. I bitched and bitched and bitched. I told my teammates I'm sorry, I don't mean to do this, but I'm going to keep talking till they just can't stand me here any more.

Some of my teammates loved it. "Right on," they said.

I quieted down. I didn't say a word when we lost the opening game to Los Angeles. I didn't say a word when we beat Atlanta in overtime in the second. We only scored one touchdown in each game, but I didn't say a word. In public.

CONKS After I left the Giants, I returned to Annapolis for a few days, then was assigned to HC-6, a helicopter combat support squadron based in Norfolk. I was miserable in Norfolk. There were too many guys there who said I'd never be a pro football player, too many guys who thought all I wanted was to get out of the navy. The truth was the navy wanted me out. Everybody wanted me out except Commodore Ustick. He wanted me in Guantanamo. At least that hadn't happened.

Kit spoke to his commanding officer in Pensacola, and after a brief stay in Norfolk, I was transferred to HC-16, Kit's squadron.

I hadn't flown in more than a year. I was going to go through a flight refresher course.

SIMMS I behaved pretty well for a while. I did my job, kept my mouth shut, took a few practice snaps every now and then with the offense, imitated Danny White of the Cowboys for the benefit of the defense, nothing real difficult for $250,000 a year. "I'm going to sit here and make the most of it," I told the reporters.

Fishof said the right things, too. "He told the coach he wants to be part of the team," David told the press, once he realized he wasn't having much luck getting me traded to Houston or anybody else. "Phil's a competitor, and that's the mark of a great quarterback, and that was the cause of his initial reaction, his great competitiveness," David added.

Then we played the Cowboys in Dallas. They were leading us only 14–13 midway through the fourth quarter when Brunner threw a screen pass that Dexter Clinksdale intercepted and ran back about seventy yards for a touchdown. Scott sort of hobbled off the field after the play, and Parcells turned to me and told me to loosen up, to get ready to go in.

I'd been ready for about three weeks.

I figured I had enough time to rally us, to get us a couple of touchdowns, or a touchdown and a field goal, enough to win the game for us. I still had my confidence. But then we fumbled the kickoff, and one of their guys picked it up and ran in for a touchdown, and the score was 28–13, and I knew I could forget about the heroics, we weren't going to catch up. The whole thing was meaningless. I really didn't want to go in.

But I did, completed a few passes, moved us all right, then threw an interception on our last play of the game.

"When are you going to make the decision to start playing me?" I asked Parcells a few days later. "You know, this is stupid."

"Phil, I have got to give the guy a chance," Parcells said. "I made the decision, I've got to live with it for a while. But it's not etched in stone."

"Okay," I said, "but, you know, you can't wait too long."

78

I was real brave with my words, but I don't think I frightened the coach.

CONKS Sharon was the most beautiful girl I'd ever met. I met her only a few weeks after I returned to Pensacola. Her father was a retired navy captain, a former pilot. It was her beauty that attracted me to her—she was a stunning blonde—but it was her sensitivity and her intelligence that made me fall in love with her. She was the second real love of my life, after Connie. Sharon was as close to perfect as anyone could be.

The doctor who gave me a physical exam before I started the refresher course asked me about my seasickness. "Did you ever have trouble in the air?" he said.

I told him I had. I told him about the times I'd gotten sick in flight school.

The doctor wanted me to undergo a desensitizing course, a course where they spin you around in chairs, turn you upside down, things like that, trying to get you accustomed to fighting off dizziness. But the people who ran the course tested me and decided my problem was too severe, I wasn't even a candidate for desensitizing. They sent me back to the doctor.

He knew that if he judged me physically fit to fly again, and if I ever had an accident, he could be in trouble. He didn't want to take any chances. He stamped me NPQ—not physically qualified to fly. He grounded me, which meant that my commitment to the navy reverted back to five years from my graduation. Instead of getting out in January 1986, five years after I received my wings, I was going to get out in May 1984.

I was going to get another chance with the Giants.

SIMMS I kept telling myself that sooner or later they'd have to give me another chance, and when they did, I had to be ready. I didn't get a chance in our fourth game, against Green Bay. Scott played a very conservative game, our running backs

gained more than 200 yards and I watched us beat the Packers.

The next week, I went into George Young's office.
"You've got to get me out of here," I said. "I just hate it.
I'm miserable. I can't stand practice. It's stupid. Why would
you even want me around here?"

George was very diplomatic. "I'll do what I can," he told
me.

Scott had a big game against San Diego. He completed
thirty-one of fifty-one passes for 395 yards and three touchdowns, and if he hadn't fumbled twice, once at the San Diego
5-yard line and once in the final minute at the San Diego 12,
we might have pulled out the game. The Chargers won, 41–
34. There were ninety-two passes thrown in the game, and I
hadn't thrown any of them.

I exploded the next day. I filled the reporters' notebooks. I
told them it was obvious the Giants were committed to Scott
Brunner as their quarterback, and I wanted to leave, I wanted
to go somewhere else, anywhere else. I told them I'd be more
comfortable somewhere else, I'd be happier, I'd have no re-
grets whatsoever about leaving the Giants. The trade deadline
was coming up in eight days, and I wanted to be traded.

"Maybe my wish will come true," Fishof said. "Maybe
Phil's wish will come true."

Our wishes didn't come true.

The following Sunday, the day before the trade deadline,
we played Philadelphia. The Eagles were ahead, 14–6, in the
third quarter, when Scott threw an interception. The crowd
was chanting, "We want Simms, we want Simms." Parcells
turned to me. "Warm up," he said.

I said, "What?"

I had my baseball cap on. I wasn't even thinking about
getting into the game.

"Go warm up," he said. "You're going in."

I started throwing on the sidelines, and the crowd went

nuts. They were cheering for me. They loved me. I hadn't thrown an interception in Giants Stadium in two years.

I went in and completed four passes in a row and marched us straight down the field for a touchdown. We held the Eagles and got the ball back and I knew I was going to do it again. But on third-and-two at our own 28-yard line, I spotted John Mistler near the sidelines, threw for him and missed him, my first incompletion. As I followed through, I brought my hand down and Dennis Harrison of the Eagles brought his arm up. My hand and his arm collided, and I said, "Damn, that hurt," and then looked down and saw the bone sticking out of my right thumb, and I said, "Holy shit, oh my God," and I started screaming. I ran and staggered to the sidelines and sort of sagged to my knees, and Ronnie Barnes, our trainer, took one look and began helping me to the locker room. My whole hand was covered with blood, and all I could think, through the pain, was, *There goes another year.*

In the locker room, Dr. Kim Sloan, our orthopedic surgeon, tried to pop the bone back into place, and he was having a terrible time with it, and he said, "Ronnie, if I don't get this back in, we've got to rush him to the hospital. I'll have to operate immediately." Finally he popped it back in, and he was so proud. "I almost gave up," he said. "I'm glad I didn't." We always made fun of Dr. Sloan, got on him about the way he talked, sort of like Elmer Fudd. We kidded him about his Wolex watch and his Fewawi automobile, but he was a genius, he was a great doctor.

I didn't have to be operated on, but I did have to go to the hospital, for observation and treatment for shock. I had what they called a compound fracture dislocation of the right thumb. Back at Giants Stadium, after losing to Philadelphia, 17–13, Scott Brunner was complaining to the press about being taken out of the game.

I was out for the season. The swelling didn't go down for months. That made four seasons in a row cut short by injuries, and I was fed up. I hit bottom. I thought I'd never get a chance to show what I knew I could do. I even told David Fishof, "This is just not going to work out."

One of the New York sportswriters wrote a column about me and said, "Maybe it is time he began to look around for another line of work."

CONKS When I heard about Simms's thumb, I just thought, *How much more can the guy take?* I knew his whole history, the knee, the shoulder, everything. I kind of doubted we'd ever play together.

I knew he had to be at rock bottom, first not starting, then getting hurt, and the team playing so badly. A couple of days later, driving to work at the base, I listened to a Norman Vincent Peale tape on positive thinking—Pete McCulley, Kit's dad, used to go to Norman Vincent Peale's church, and he gave us a whole collection of the tapes—and I really wanted to send it to Simms. I figured if anybody ever needed it, he needed it then.

I followed the Giants pretty carefully all through the season. I felt I was still part of the team. I was on military reserve. They hadn't waived me. I watched them on "Monday Night Football" against St. Louis, and I was cheering for their rookie kicker, Ali Haji-Sheikh, when he tried to break a 20–20 tie with a 66-yard field goal on the last play of overtime. He missed what would have been the longest field goal in NFL history, ending his streak of fourteen successful field goal attempts in a row.

I was really impressed by Haji-Sheikh. He kicked thirty-five field goals—an NFL record—in forty-two attempts. He made two 56-yarders. He kicked four field goals in one game against Seattle and five in the next game against Washington. He played in the Pro Bowl as a rookie. I figured place-kicking was the one thing the Giants didn't have to worry about for a long time.

A couple of times during the season, I called John Mistler, just to hear some inside gossip. He'd been friendly during training camp, as friendly as veterans can be when they're not sure whether you're going to make the team, and he was having a real good season. He caught eight passes one game. I called mostly to ask him about the two wide receivers the Giants picked up, Mike Miller in the middle of the season and Byron Williams near the end.

I figured two more wideouts just made it that much more difficult for me to make the team in 1984. But Mistler was encouraging. He thought if I worked as hard as I had in 1983, I could win a spot.

SIMMS We won only one game the rest of the season. We wound up with three victories, twelve defeats and one tie, our worst record since I'd become a Giant. Scott had to listen to the boos, and so did Parcells. Scott played himself right out of his job—he was traded after the season—and Parcells almost coached himself out of his. There were very strong rumors that George Young was talking to an old friend, Howard Schnellenberger, the University of Miami coach, about coming to the Giants. But somehow Parcells survived. George Young gave him one more chance to make us into winners, and I got another chance, too.

CONKS When I went home for Christmas, one of my cousins, a girl named Kris Ann Piazza, told me she thought I had a lot of courage to try out for the National Football League. She said I was an inspiration to her.

Kris Ann is a quadriplegic. In 1979, when she was twelve, she dove into a swimming pool and broke her neck, and she's been in a wheelchair ever since. She's undergone dozens of operations, most of them terribly painful, trying to regain some use of her body and her senses.

She can hold some things, but she can't manipulate them. She's not supposed to have any feeling below her chest, but if you tickle her feet, she smiles. She feels things. She just can't move.

We're second cousins, but we've gotten close in recent years. Whenever I feel like letting up, or complaining, I think about her and what she goes through every day of her life.

I told Kris Ann she was an inspiration to me.

1984

In which McConkey makes his NFL
debut, and Simms makes his
comeback

■ In 1983, twenty-five New York Giants spent all or part of
the season on injured reserve. In 1984, Bill Parcells decided
he needed a strength-and-conditioning coach, a job that had
been vacant for a few seasons. "You know anybody?" he
asked Bobby Knight, the Indiana University basketball
coach.

Parcells and Knight had both coached at West Point when
they were younger and thinner. Their friendship, and their
waistlines, had flourished for two decades.

Knight recommended Johnny Parker, who had once been
the strength-and-conditioning coach at Indiana. "Where's he
now?" Parcells asked.

"Ole Miss," Knight said.

Coincidentally, the head football coach at the University of
Mississippi was Steve Sloan, for whom Parcells had been defensive coordinator at Vanderbilt and at Texas Tech. Sloan
spoke highly of Parker, and Parcells hired him.

Parker, earnest, dedicated, enthusiastic, likable, had earned an official master's degree at Delta State University and an unofficial doctorate in Moscow. He had studied with some of the best coaches and trainers in the Soviet Union, and he believed not in their methods, but in their findings.

"I can't experiment on my players," Parker says. "But they can, and they do. If it doesn't work, they just bury that guy, and run another one in. The things they tell us are tried and true. They *work.*"

Parker's assignment, basically, was to make the Giants strong and keep them healthy. "I don't think there have to be injuries in football," he says. "If you train rationally, and your lifestyle's in order, you're eating the right things and getting the right amount of sleep, you ought not to get hurt."

Parker found that not many of the Giants knew how to weight-train rationally. "The ones that really wanted to do it were doing too much," he says, "and the others had no idea what to do." He started an off-season weightlifting and conditioning program in April 1984.

In 1984, only six New York Giants spent all or part of the season on injured reserve.

Johnny Parker's weight room, modernized for the 1985 season, became a sanctuary for the Giants, a refuge where they stretched and strained, beyond the brink of pain and fatigue, and still found the energy to needle—and to appreciate—each other.

For Phil Simms and Phil McConkey, the weight room soon became a second home. "A fun place," Simms called it.

SIMMS As soon as Johnny Parker joined us, I went to him and said I wanted to start working out with him. "Aw gee, Phil," he said—he really does talk that way—"Aw gee, Phil, I'm awfully sorry, but I just don't have a program for quarterbacks yet. I just scratched one out for the linemen. Will you give me a couple of days?"

"Hell, no," I said. "I'll do what the linemen do."

I still do. We lift different amounts of weights, of course, but the principles are the same. The percentages of capability are the same.

In the spring of 1984, I practically lived in Giants Stadium. When I wasn't stretching or lifting, I was sitting in an office with Ron Erhardt. We watched more films than I had ever watched before. There was a real sense of urgency for everybody involved, for me, for Ron, for Parcells. Our jobs were at stake. If we didn't go out and get it done, we knew there were going to be new people around.

It wasn't a question of learning technical things from the films, of learning to recognize different kinds of defenses, for instance, and where they're vulnerable. It was more a question of making sure that Ron and I were on the same page mentally. We got to know each other better than ever. We got to understand each other. We were working to get to the point where I would know what he was thinking, and he would know what I was thinking, where we could communicate almost without saying a word.

We knew that we finally had a chance to do with the offense what Ron really wanted to do. It hadn't been his philosophy up till then, not the year he spent under Perkins, not the first year under Parcells. Bill wanted a high-percentage offense that first year: Run and throw it short. But after the season was over, Bill decided he didn't like that. "Hell," he told us, "if we're gonna throw it, let's throw it downfield."

That was always Ron's philosophy. Mine, too. We stuck to that philosophy through training camp, through the exhibition season, through the regular season, and it worked for us. It got us into the playoffs. A couple of years later, it got us into the Super Bowl. There are days when it doesn't work, but it keeps getting better and better.

CONKS I was working out in Pensacola the only way I knew how—too hard, running too many sprints, lifting too much weight, diving for passes from Kit McCulley and from a more experienced quarterback who was living in the neighborhood, Richard Todd, who'd been traded from the New York Jets to the New Orleans Saints.

I kept scoring imaginary touchdowns, and, after each one, I practiced spiking the ball.

I was working on my relationship with Sharon, too. I loved her as much as I loved football.

Almost.

SIMMS I knew I was in trouble before we even started running. Bernard King was six-foot-seven, and Jan Van Breda Kolff, his ex-teammate, was six-foot-eight, and both of them weighed less than I did. I couldn't believe how skinny they were. Still, I hate to lose—at anything—and I kept thinking I'd just try to stay close to those guys, save something for a late move, then pass them.

Sure.

Diana and I had just moved to Franklin Lakes, and both Van Breda Kolff, who'd finished his career in the National Basketball Association, and King, who was the star of the New York Knicks, lived close by. Van Breda Kolff had seen me running, as part of my pre-training-camp conditioning program, and he asked me if I wanted to run with him and Bernard. I was pretty excited about it. I was a big fan of King's.

"We'll just go a couple of times around the reservoir," Jan said, "and then up that hill and then we'll rest a while and then run a little more."

There was no way they were going to let some football player outrun them. We ran two or maybe three miles around the reservoir, and by the time we started up the hill, I knew I was beaten. I had nothing left for a late move.

I thought I'd never reach the top, but I did, and Jan was waiting for me. "We're gonna take a break now, Phil, okay?" he said. I nodded, and about ten seconds later, he said,

"Okay, ready to go now?" Actually, the break lasted three or four minutes, but it felt like ten seconds. We ran down the hill and around the reservoir a couple of more times, and I decided that in the future, I'd run by myself or with a couple of my linemen. Benson maybe, and Ard.

Van Breda Kolff and another one of his former teammates, Maurice Lucas, who was six-foot-nine, came over to the high school field and caught passes from me. They were great targets. They spoiled me. They had to reach down to catch balls McConkey would've had to leap for.

CONKS The Giants gave me a $10,000 raise. When I signed the contract in 1983 for $45,000, they told me they'd pay me $55,000 for my second year, and even though I didn't play in 1983, the Giants still agreed to give me $55,000 in 1984—provided, of course, that I made the team.

SIMMS Before we went to training camp, the Giants offered me a three-year contract worth more than a million dollars, which wasn't exactly unfair, considering that I'd only played in two out of thirty-two games going back to 1981. If it had been up to me, I probably would've taken it. Anything over ten dollars an hour still sounds like a lot to me.

But that's what I've got David Fishof for, to save me from myself. He did his research as usual, saw what other quarterbacks were getting, and then he asked me if I wanted to gamble. Does a Bear play in Chicago?

He told me that if I didn't take the Giants' offer, I could play out my option in 1984—play for my 1983 salary plus 10 percent, which would come to $275,000—and then negotiate a new salary in 1985, based on my performance. If I had a big year in 1984, I'd be in a strong bargaining position. "We could shoot for the moon," David said.

Of course, if I had a poor year, or got hurt again, I'd be in a weak position. I love to gamble, especially on my own skills, and I could tell that David wanted to gamble, too. "Let's go for it," I told him. "Let's play out the option."

Pretty cocky, huh, for a guy who hadn't started a game in three years?

I'd always heard that it took two years for a knee to heal properly after surgery. When I went back in 1983, I thought I was ready to go, but maybe I wasn't. Maybe the broken thumb was a blessing in disguise. Maybe it gave my knee the time it needed to heal. In 1984, I threw away the heavy knee brace I wore the year before. My knee was healed.

Coach Parcells said at the beginning of training camp that the starting quarterback would be either Jeff Rutledge or me. Jeff started four games in 1983, after I got hurt, and he threw more passes, completed more passes and gained more yardage in those four games than in all the rest of his professional career.

His career began when mine did, in 1979. He was drafted in the ninth round, out of Alabama, by the Los Angeles Rams. He was a backup quarterback for the Rams for three years before he became a backup quarterback for us.

I thought I could beat out Jeff as long as I stayed healthy. I heard stories about the Giant fans who were running pools on when I'd get hurt this time. I sure wasn't the golden boy anymore. The fans and the media weren't counting on me to turn the franchise around.

CONKS In our opening exhibition game, Simms stepped into the starting lineup for the first time in two years and played as if he'd never been away. We beat New England, 48–20, and he completed ten of fourteen passes, three for touchdowns, to tight end Zeke Mowatt, to Bobby Johnson and to me.

Bobby Johnson, from Kansas University, was a rookie, a free agent, like me, about an inch taller and a couple of pounds heavier. You could tell he was a football player from day one. You could see he had a feel for the game, a feel for beating defensive backs, a feel for running patterns. He had all the right instincts.

The competition among the wide receivers was brutal. We had another rookie, Lionel Manuel, from the University of the Pacific, who showed tremendous quickness and incredible cuts. Bobby Johnson and I agreed we would break our ankles if we tried to make the cuts Lionel made.

We also had Earnest Gray, who in 1983, in his fifth NFL season, led the league in receptions, plus three other veterans: Mike Miller, a speed burner; Byron Williams, who was cut by Green Bay in 1983 and picked up by the Giants late in the season, in time to catch twenty passes in the last four games; and John Mistler, my roommate in training camp.

Three strong rookies and four talented veterans—and only five of us were going to make the team.

"I got guys that have been around here," Pat Hodgson told us rookies, "but I'm not married to them, you know. If you're better, you're going to be here."

Mistler, who played for Arizona State, had been with the Giants for three seasons. He caught more then forty passes in 1983. He was my best friend on the team. He put up with my weird sleeping habits, and he was always willing to help me, to go over plays or techniques with me.

In a sense, I was trying to take food off his table, but I didn't wish any bad things on him, and I'm positive he didn't wish any on me. I wanted to catch every single ball that was thrown to me, but I didn't wish for him or Lionel or Bobby or anyone else to miss any balls that were thrown to them.

I wanted to win a job because of my performance, not because someone else did poorly. That's not being a winner. There's no glory in that, and no fun. Being a winner is concentrating on yourself, doing everything within your power to succeed, doing everything to the best of your ability.

That's the only way to win.

SIMMS Parcells made his decision early. He named me as the starting quarterback after our second exhibition game. Jeff was upset, of course, although he handled the disappointment a lot better than I had in 1983. I was delighted. Finally, I felt I could relax, be myself, play my game.

I was playing with a lightweight knee brace, and neither the knee nor the brace gave me any trouble. The thumb was healed, the shoulder was strong and my head was healthy, too. I felt that I knew what I was doing on the field.

The day Parcells gave me the starting job, the captain of our defense, Harry Carson, walked out of training camp, angry and frustrated. He didn't want to play for the Giants anymore. I could understand how he felt. Harry joined the Giants in 1976, out of South Carolina State, intelligent, articulate, a natural leader, a gifted athlete. He'd already played in five Pro Bowls, but he'd played on only one winning Giant team. As talented as he was, he hated losing.

After the 1983 season, after two of his fellow linebackers, Brad Van Pelt and Brian Kelley, were traded away, Harry demanded to be traded, too. Before his skills faded, he wanted to play on a winner. He wanted to play in a Super Bowl. He figured he didn't have a chance in New York.

CONKS Harry Carson came back to camp a few days later, cheerful and ready to play. "Just my annual training-camp vacation," Carson explained. I'd hardly noticed he was gone, I was so wrapped up in my own survival. They cut Mike Miller, which left six wide receivers competing for five positions.

I got out to the stadium early, as usual, several hours before we were to play Pittsburgh in our final exhibition game. I was sitting on a stool in the almost-empty locker room when Parcells came up to me and said, "You've made this team. I want you to go out tonight and relax and just play your ass off. You're a hell of a kid, and I'm glad you're with us."

Relax? I wanted to jump up and scream and yell and run around the locker room. I wanted to tell everyone in New York and Buffalo and Washington and Annapolis and Pensacola and Norfolk that I was a New York Giant.

But I just smiled and said, "Thank you, Coach," and then I went out and played my ass off. I caught three passes and I took one punt back 48 yards, just missed breaking it for a touchdown.

We beat the Steelers on an 87-yard pass play from Jeff Rutledge to Byron Williams in the last couple of minutes, improved our exhibition record to three-and-one, and afterward I went back to my hotel room and I closed the door and I started to cry, I was so happy, I was so proud of what I had done.

I was in the National Football League.

I was about to play my first official football game in almost six years.

I had dinner the following night at John Mistler's house, with his wife and his children and his parents, and just before we sat down to eat, the phone rang. John answered it, and when he got off, you could tell he wasn't happy. It was one of Parcells's assistants; the coach wanted to see him the next day.

When they met, Parcells told John he'd been cut, he'd been placed on waivers. I saw John as he was leaving the locker room, and I asked him what happened, and he told me, and I didn't know what to say. I just wished him luck. I had such mixed emotions. I was so happy about making the team myself, and yet I felt so bad that John was leaving, partly because of me.

I really think that Byron Williams beat out Mistler by making the catch that won the game against Pittsburgh. I don't think it came down to John and me. But I'll never know for sure.

* * *

Simms made his return official when we opened the season against Philadelphia in Giants Stadium—and he made it sensational. He completed twenty-three of thirty passes for 409 yards and four touchdowns and no interceptions. He threw two touchdown passes to Bobby Johnson, one to Zeke Mowatt and one to Byron Williams, just enough for us to beat the Eagles by one point.

Scott Brunner never had a game like that.

Hardly anyone ever did.

SIMMS The second game, we beat Dallas, 28–7, and I threw three more touchdown passes and, again, no interceptions. It was the first time in sixteen years the Giants had won two in a row at the start of a season, and I loved every minute of it.

In the two victories, I threw two touchdown passes to Zeke Mowatt, two to Byron Williams, two to Bobby Johnson and one to Lionel Manuel, all receivers I was working with regularly for the first time. Johnson and Manuel were both rookie wideouts with worlds of talent. I knew I'd be passing to them for a long time.

I had better receivers than I'd ever had before, and I also had better blocking. In earlier years, the only way I could tell whether I'd thrown a completion or an interception most of the time was by the reaction of the crowd. I was flat on my back listening.

But in 1984 we had two big rookies starting at the tackles, Karl Nelson from Iowa State and Bill Roberts from Ohio State, and two veterans at the guards, Billy Ard and Brad Benson, and Kevin Belcher at center, and they were giving me the kind of protection I'd always wanted. I actually saw most of my passes being caught.

I saw more before I threw the ball, too. I looked for more receivers. I'd spent so much time during the spring watching films with Ron Erhardt that I'd learned to read the defenses better.

I was turning into a pretty good quarterback, and we were turning into a pretty good team.

CONKS In a way, I was more in awe of Ron Erhardt than I was of Parcells. Erhardt had been the head coach of the New England Patriots, in the same division with the Buffalo Bills. That impressed me. I listened to Erhardt, and I learned a lot. I learned that he was an instigator. He'd get me to get on Simms, and then he'd get Simms to get on me. He was a yeller, too, like Parcells. Pat Hodgson never yelled, never raised his voice. That impressed me, too.

SIMMS Two days after we beat Dallas, my fan club expanded. My daughter Deirdre was born. Diana had to have a cesarean section, so for good luck she chose to deliver on the date in September—the eleventh—that matched my uniform number.

The baby was healthy, and so was Diana. I was on a winning streak off the field, too.

CONKS I'd played only on special teams in the first two games. I hadn't played a down offensively. But when Earnest Gray hurt his shoulder in the first quarter against the Washington Redskins, Pat Hodgson turned to me and said, "You go in." He gave me the play—a "go" pattern.

My first play from scrimmage. I was nervous as hell. We were on their 35-yard line. I was on the left side. I raced straight down the field, looked over my inside shoulder, saw the pass was going to my outside, spun my head—and dove.

I caught the ball a foot off the ground. We were inside the one-yard line. Rob Carpenter went in for the touchdown.

I played the rest of the game, caught two more passes— Simms threw for more than 300 yards—and we almost made it three straight victories. We led the Redskins, 14–13, going into the final quarter. But three turnovers—two fumbles and an interception—led to a field goal and two touchdowns for Washington, and the Redskins beat us, 30–14. They had played in the previous two Super Bowls.

In our fourth game, I returned a punt 31 yards to set up a field goal, and then Simms threw two touchdown passes and we beat Tampa Bay, 17–14. I felt like I was really contributing.

We went into Los Angeles with three victories and one defeat, and when we kicked off to start the game, we called "deep kick right," which meant that I was the force guy, I had to sprint like hell to force the returner to the center of the field. Their returner lost the ball in the sun, and it began bouncing around, and he ignored it, and as I sprinted downfield, a light went off in my head: *After ten yards, it's a free ball. After ten yards, it's a free ball.* I fell on the free ball in the end zone for the first touchdown of my professional career and one of the fastest in the history of the NFL. One of my dreams had come true, but the rest of the game was a nightmare.

Simms got sacked five times. We had two punts blocked. We gave up three safeties. And I fumbled the ball away on a kickoff return for the first time in my life. It was late in the game and we were way behind, and I got stood up by about six guys, and they stripped me of the ball.

I also came out of the game with a slash on my chin. I was running a "go" pattern, racing down the sidelines, and I saw the Rams had me covered outside. So I veered to the inside, and I knew I had the cornerback beat, but as I went up for the catch, as I was in midair, Nolan Cromwell, the safety, came over from the far side and plowed into me, drove his helmet up into my chin. I was wearing a soft chin strap instead of the normal hard kind, and the soft strap didn't offer much protection. Cromwell slammed me to the ground, and when I got up and undid the strap, the whole area was covered with blood.

I needed eight stitches to close it up—after the game.

Midway through the season, the day after we lost to Philadelphia, evening our record at four and four, Rob Carpenter, the running back, our leading rusher, was out on the practice field early, talking to Parcells, talking *at* Parcells. He kept jabbing his index finger in Parcells's direction to make his point. "You got to use McConkey more," Carpenter said. "The guy can play."

Carpenter was my roommate on road trips, and my biggest fan. He always pumped me. He told me I had a rare combination of speed and quickness. He was never fooled. He never believed the stereotype of the white receiver with the big heart and the slow feet. Some people made it sound as if I was just one big heart on the field. A heart with no skills, no talent, no arms, no legs, just a heart. Carpenter knew I was more than that. He knew I could run.

Parcells respected Carpenter's judgment. Everybody respected Carpenter's judgment. He'd played with strong teams in Houston, playoff teams, before he became a Giant, and in Houston, he told me, "They won with character players. Maybe not as much talent as some teams, but a lot of character. That's what you win with."

Parcells used me more the next game. I had caught only one pass in the previous five games, but against Washington I caught two passes, both against double coverage in key situations. Once, on third and three, Simms and I teamed up for 39 yards down to the Redskins' 5-yard line, and the other time, on third and five, we gained 23 yards, again down to the five. The two receptions set up two of Joe Morris's three touchdown runs, the first big day of his Giants career.

Simms had a big day, too, eighteen for twenty-nine for 339

yards, no interceptions and two touchdowns, one to Earnest Gray, who caught seven passes.

We beat the Redskins, 37–13, the first of five victories in six games, a streak that lifted us toward the playoffs. The Giants had been in the playoffs only once, in 1981, in the previous twenty years.

SIMMS The fans in Giants Stadium gave us a huge ovation when we beat Washington, and I thought we deserved it. The thirty-seven points we scored against the Redskins—after we'd lost to them six times in a row—were the most we'd scored in a game in four years.

Jim Burt and Lawrence Taylor were so excited they decided to celebrate by pouring a bucket of ice water on Parcells. For once, Parcells didn't yell at Burt, probably because he was afraid Lawrence might think he was yelling at him. Parcells didn't know the shower was going to become a ritual, a symbol of our success, two years later.

Chris Godfrey moved into the offensive line in the Washington game, at right guard, replacing Brad Benson, who moved to left tackle, replacing Bill Roberts, who was injured. Godfrey was a real find. He started in the NFL as a defensive tackle in 1980, spent time with the Redskins, the Jets and the Packers, then jumped to the United States Football League and became an offensive lineman. I don't know how George Young spotted him, but he did. Chris did a great job against Washington. He kept Dave Butz away from my body.

In the locker room, after the game, I yelled, "We ought to get two days off for this one," and the other guys picked it up and began chanting, "Two days off! Two days off!" Finally, Parcells said, "Okay, you guys can have Monday and Tuesday off"—everybody cheered—"but you better play your asses off next week."

The following week, we beat Dallas, the first time we'd defeated the Cowboys twice in one season since 1963, and

Parcells said we could have two days off again. We've had Mondays and Tuesdays off ever since, although a lot of us go in on our own, to lift weights or to run or stretch or at least get some steam to take the sting out of the wounds.

After Dallas, we split games with Tampa Bay and St. Louis. Then we played Kansas City at Giants Stadium, and by half-time I'd thrown three interceptions, and the fans were booing me about as loudly as they'd been cheering a month earlier.

The Chiefs were ahead, 27–14, in the fourth quarter. Then, in the last nine minutes, I completed eight of ten passes for 155 yards and two touchdowns, and we overtook them and beat them, 28–27, and our loyal fans loved me again.

So did Parcells. "Phil's a fighter, a bull rider," the coach said.

CONKS I wasn't on the field for Simms's heroics. For me, the Kansas City game ended in the first few minutes.

I made the tackle on the opening kickoff, and then after three downs, the Chiefs punted. I took the punt and started up the sidelines. I could've stepped out after a few yards, but I knew that if I put my head down and drove forward, I could get three or four extra yards.

I drove forward, and after I was knocked down, one of the Chiefs landed on my back and his helmet dug into me and rammed my ribs into the ground.

You don't get hurt badly when you get hit in midair, when you're not offering any resistance. You don't get hurt badly by a tackle. You get hurt badly by hitting *against* something, like the ground.

The play ended not far from our bench, and I sort of bounced up from force of habit, not really feeling the pain yet, and Parcells said, "You all right?"

I could barely answer. "Wind," I managed to say.

I figured I'd had the wind knocked out of me, I'd catch my breath and I'd go back in. But I couldn't catch my breath. I couldn't straighten up. I kept leaning to the side. I told Ronnie Barnes, our trainer, how I felt, and he checked me out and found that I had four broken ribs.

I don't mind playing with one or two cracked ribs, the kind that make it painful to cough or laugh or sneeze—you have to play with them—but this time not only were four broken, but one of them was displaced. If I took one good hit, Ronnie told me, I could have a punctured lung.

Outside of Ronnie and Parcells, nobody seemed to notice I was hurt. The public-address announcer didn't say a word. Sharon had come up from Pensacola to see me play for the first time, and my folks had come down from Buffalo, and they all kept wondering why I wasn't returning punts anymore.

I was in the hospital for two days with a hemothorax. I had two pints of blood coagulated in my lung area. The blood finally dissipated, which was a relief because then they didn't have to poke a hole in me and insert a tube to bring out the blood.

Sharon came to see me in the hospital, and I told her how lonely I'd been all season without her. I told her how much I loved her. I asked her to marry me.

She hesitated, but she said yes.

We were engaged. We were going to get married in the spring of 1985.

I couldn't laugh, but I was smiling.

The doctors decided I was out for the rest of the season. Earnest Gray was already on injured reserve, so we were down to three healthy wide receivers—Lionel Manuel, Bobby Johnson and Byron Williams. We had to have a fourth wideout—and John Mistler was the perfect candidate.

Buffalo had signed John after Parcells had cut him. Then the Bills had cut him, too. He was available and he knew our system.

John was signed to take my place, and he moved into my house, a house in Clifton, New Jersey, that I'd been sharing with two defensive veterans, Dee Hardison and Kenny Hill. Dee played for the Bills when I was in college, and Kenny played for the Raiders in two Super Bowls.

We were eight-and-five, with three games to go. We had a shot at the Super Bowl. A long shot.

SIMMS Two days before we played the New York Jets, I ordered twenty pizzas and half a dozen two-foot hero sandwiches for lunch, and I wasn't even full. I bought the food for the whole team.

The year before, when I was hurt, we picked up a third-string quarterback named Tom Owens, who was so happy to be in the NFL that he bought lunch for everybody every Friday. When Tom left, he told me, "It's your ball now. Keep the tradition going."

I did. I didn't want any starving blockers in front of me.

We beat the Jets, 20–10, and with two games to go, we were in first place in the National Football Conference East. Washington and Dallas were also in first place. We all had nine victories and five defeats. St. Louis, at eight-and-six, was also in contention for a berth in the playoffs.

Then we played the Cardinals, and even though I threw a couple of touchdown passes and Joe Morris rushed for more than 100 yards for the first time in his three years as a pro, St. Louis came from behind—Neil Lomax had a hell of a game—and beat us, 31–21. We not only lost the game. We lost two starters, cornerback Mark Haynes and guard Billy Ard, both injured and out for the rest of the season.

Washington beat Dallas and moved into first place all alone at ten-and-five. The Cowboys and the Cardinals shared second place with us.

Everything came down to the final week of the regular season. Ironically, our game, against New Orleans, on Saturday, meant absolutely nothing. Whether we won or lost, St. Louis still had to lose on Sunday *and* Dallas had to lose on Monday for us to get into the playoffs as a wild-card team. It was all pretty complicated, but that's what it came down to.

We were all very depressed because we'd gotten ourselves into a situation where everything was out of our control. We felt helpless. We just went through the motions against New Orleans. We were so bad that *I* was the leading rusher. I outgained both Morris and Carpenter. We lost, 10–3. The game was at Giants Stadium, and even our fans were out of it. They were too bored to boo.

Then we waited.

On Sunday, the Cardinals played the Redskins in Washington, and I watched the game on TV in my family room. I was up and down the whole day. I couldn't stay still and I couldn't eat, I was so nervous. I must've lost five pounds that weekend. The Redskins took a 23–7 lead at halftime, but then Lomax went crazy. He couldn't miss. He completed twenty-five of twenty-eight passes in the second half, or something unbelievable like that, and I kept cussing at the Washington defense and screaming, "Stop him! Stop him!"

With about six minutes to play, Lomax threw a touchdown pass to Roy Green, and the Cardinals went ahead, 27–26, and I ran into the kitchen and told Diana, who was suffering too, "Do you believe this? I know the Redskins are going to lose."

But with a minute and a half to go, Mark Moseley kicked a field goal that lifted Washington to a 29–27 victory.

We were still alive.

On Monday night, the Cowboys played the Dolphins in Miami, and I was in front of the TV again. I would've been watching even if we were in last place. I haven't missed watching a Monday-night game since God knows when. Fishof knows I don't do engagements on Monday nights because I don't want to miss the game. I'm a fan.

I cheered for Dan Marino, who threw two touchdown passes to give Miami a 14–0 lead in the third quarter. But then Dallas came back, scored twice and tied the game at 14–14. Marino threw another touchdown pass, but then Tony Hill caught a deflected pass and went about 60 yards for a touchdown that tied the score at 21–21. I walked out of the room. I couldn't watch.

With less than a minute to play, Marino threw his fourth touchdown pass, his third to Mark Clayton, a 61-yard play that put Miami in front, 28–21.

CONKS I was watching the game with John Mistler and Dee Hardison, and when the clock ran out on the Cowboys—it was probably after midnight—the three of us threw open our front door and just began screaming at the top of our lungs.

SIMMS The Dallas Cowboys were out of the playoffs, for the first time in ten years, and by the narrowest of margins, we were in—for the second time in twenty-one years.

And I was in for the first time in my career.

I spent Christmas away from home for the first time in my life, but I didn't complain. We beat the Los Angeles Rams in the wild-card playoff game, 16–13, two days before Christmas, then stayed on the West Coast to get ready to play San Francisco six days later.

The victory over the Rams, who'd beaten us badly early in the season, was a perfect Christmas present, but our season ended in San Francisco. The 49ers beat us, 21–10, and for the third time in five years, our season ended with a loss to the team that went on to win the Super Bowl.

Joe Montana was the Most Valuable Player again.

CONKS If there's one thing wrong with Simms, it's that he doesn't appreciate statistics. He doesn't even care about them. I'm hooked on statistics. I have been ever since I started following Kemp's passing and Dubenion's receiving. I know what I did every year back to my sophomore year in high school. I never had a season like Simms had in 1984.

He threw 533 passes, which set a Giants record. He completed 286, which was also a record, and he gained 4,044 yards, a third record. His four 300-yard games tied the Giants record for one season and gave him eleven for his career, which broke the record. He broke two records set by Fran Tarkenton and two by Y. A. Tittle, both of whom are in the Hall of Fame.

My statistics weren't bad for a rookie. I caught eight passes for 154 yards, returned forty-six punts for 306 yards and returned twenty-eight kickoffs for 541 yards, a total of 1,001 yards, even though I missed the last three games. I went over the 1,000-yard mark with those three or four extra yards I got on my final punt return of the year.

I thought I had a terrific season.

Simms thought his was pretty good.

SIMMS I may not be an expert on statistics, but I know this: McConkey leads the league in strikeouts. With women. He throws more passes than I do, but I don't think any of them go for touchdowns. What did he score for us in 1984? One touchdown, on a recovered fumble? That's about what he did socially, too. Till he got engaged.

1985

In which Simms to McConkey, the passing combination, finally produces a touchdown

CONKS Sharon and I set the date for April. But at the end of January we decided to call it off. We both felt we weren't sure and we didn't want to take a chance.

I still wonder why, because, in so many ways, she seemed like the perfect girl to me. I guess it was the emphasis I placed on getting to where I wanted to be, which was the Super Bowl. I was consumed by that, and I put so much into it, physically and mentally, that maybe I didn't leave enough of me for her.

I don't know. I wish we could have worked it out. I called her a few times during the 1986 season, just to say hello, and she always asked me why I was calling. She sounded as if I was intruding, and I don't know why.

I didn't have an agent my first year with the Giants, but I thought I should have one before I signed in 1985. Simms told me to call his agent, David Fishof. He said he'd tell Fishof I was going to call.

SIMMS I forgot to tell David, and after Conks called him, David called me and said, "Who's Phil McConkey?" David is not the greatest football fan in the world. "He's a nice guy," I said. "You'll like him."

"Will he amount to anything?" David asked.

"I think so," I said.

CONKS Fishof told me he was going to spring training in Florida, to Fort Lauderdale, to see Lou Piniella of the Yankees, who was one of his clients. "Why don't you come and see me in Pensacola?" I said.

SIMMS As soon as David got off the plane in Pensacola, he heard a guy say, "David Fishof?"

David looked at the guy and said, "Oh, are you gonna take me to Phil McConkey?"

"No," the guy said. "I *am* Phil McConkey."

David couldn't believe how small Conks was. He thought *I* was the smallest player in pro football.

CONKS David Fishof agreed to represent me, and by the time he went to see George Young, he knew how tall I was, how fast I was, how many punts I returned, how many kickoffs I returned, how many passes I caught and how many yards I gained. He got me a $40,000 raise.

SIMMS I was a holdout when training camp opened. Actually, Fishof was a holdout. I just did what David told me to do. I stayed home. I didn't want to. I wanted to play football. David told me I was a terrible client. "You're such a jock," he said.

Parcells called me at home the first night. "How close are you?" he asked me.

"We're getting pretty close, Bill," I said.

"How much have they offered you?" he said.

I was embarrassed, talking about money with him, and I started saying, "Well, it's a lot, you know, and—" And he said, "Well, how much is it?"

I told him, finally.

"My God, Simms!" Parcells said. "How much money do you want?"

I said, "I don't know."

He made me feel bad. I called Fishof and told him he had to get my contract settled quickly. I was packed. I was ready to go. I was driving my wife crazy.

Fishof said I was driving him crazy, too.

Two days after camp opened, Fishof and George Young reached an agreement, and about three minutes later I was in my car and on my way to Pace University in Pleasantville, New York, the site of our training camp.

I wasn't the highest-paid quarterback in the NFL, but I was getting about twice as much as I would've made if I'd signed in 1984. The newspapers said the Giants were paying me $3.8 million for five years, and they were pretty close. David told me there were some pretty good bonus clauses, too. I believed him. I didn't bother to read them.

I was happy. I figured this was my final contract. When it was over, I'd have eleven years in the NFL. There was a time when I wondered seriously if I'd have five.

CONKS The guys started teasing me in mini-camp about my broken engagement. Rob Carpenter kept reminding me that he had lost the deposit on the low-fare airline tickets he'd bought to fly to Pensacola for the wedding.

Some of the guys began calling me "Jimmy," for Jimmy Cefalo, the former wide receiver for the Miami Dolphins who'd called off his marriage the day of the wedding. He just didn't show up or something. My thing wasn't like that. We broke up two or three months before we were supposed to get married. It wasn't as if I left her at the church.

Coincidentally, Jimmy Cefalo was the guy who, when he was at Penn State, beat me out for the best punt-return average in college football.

SIMMS Lots of guys would like to end their careers in the Hall of Fame, but I almost ended mine in the Hall of Fame game. It was our opening exhibition, against Houston, part of the annual ceremonies in Canton, Ohio, and in the first quarter, on a passing play, Mike Stensrud, their nose tackle, charged up the middle, and as I let go of the ball, I followed through and caught my pinky in his face mask. The mask sliced through the skin. Blood started gushing. I thought, *Not again.*

I came off the field, and Pat Hodgson looked at my hand and almost fainted. I kept thinking that if I was hurt again, if this was going to keep me from playing for another season, I was going to quit. I wasn't going to go through this anymore. I'd finally had the kind of season I knew I was capable of having, and I wasn't going to spend any more time on the sidelines watching.

It took four stitches to stop the bleeding, but by then I knew the finger was going to be all right in a week or two; it wasn't going to affect my passing or keep me out of the regular season. I calmed down. I sat out the rest of the Hall of Fame game—we beat Houston, 21–20, the first of five straight victories in an undefeated preseason—and I missed the next exhibition, but that was all.

CONKS I raced down the right sideline, covering the kickoff, watching the returner, who was heading the other way. I never saw the guy coming at me from my right. I saw him later—on film. I just got killed, one of those knock-your-dick-off collisions.

"You're down, you're up," Romeo Crennel, our special teams coach, always preaches, and as hard as I went down, I bounced up, cut across the field and was in on the tackle.

Then I ran to the sidelines and stripped off my chin strap—
I was still wearing the soft kind that doesn't really protect you
—and the flesh came off with it, just fell right off my chin. I
felt numb.

Only a couple of minutes remained in the first half of our
second exhibition game, against Denver, so I stayed on the
sidelines till the intermission. Ronnie Barnes told me to keep
my chin strap buckled. I guess he didn't want the rest of my
chin to fall off.

At halftime, I went in the training room and lay down on
the table, and Russell Warren, the team physician, examined
me, then started stitching me up. He didn't say much. "How
is it?" I asked, and Dr. Warren said, "Oh well, we'll be able
to fix it."

Just then, Simms, who wasn't playing, walked into the
training room and came up to the table and said, "Let me see,
Doc."

Dr. Warren stepped back, and Simms leaned over me and
let out a little yell. "Holy shit," he said. "That looks terrible."

"Thanks, Phil," Dr. Warren said. "We're trying to down-
play this thing."

"Well, what is it?" I said.

"It's pretty bad," Dr. Warren said. "But I'll do my best to
put it together."

There wasn't much he could do. It wasn't as though it was
a cut and he could sew it together. There was a big gap. What
do you sew?

I got another sixteen stitches, right on top of the eight from
the year before against the Rams.

I've got a scar now right under the cleft in my chin, but it's
okay. The women seem to like it.

At the end of training camp, Ronnie Barnes, our trainer,
told me I could stay at his house in East Brunswick, New

Jersey, for a few days while I looked for a place of my own. I moved in, and I never moved out, not till the season was over. I offered to pay rent, but Ronnie wouldn't take anything.

Ronnie Barnes is a very bright and unusual human being. He's got his master's degree from Michigan State University, and he's one of the few black head trainers in professional sports. In 1983, not long after he turned thirty, he was named by his fellow trainers the Professional Sports Trainer of the Year.

The fact that Ronnie is black made absolutely no difference to me, and the fact that I'm white made no difference to him. I'm color-blind, and always have been. My roommate at Annapolis, A. B. Miller, was black. I don't think there's any racial tension on the Giants, just a lot of racial teasing. The black guys keep asking Lamar Leachman, our defensive line coach, who's from Georgia originally and sounds it, where he gets his sheets laundered. Of course, among his linemen, Lamar's got a black guy who's married to a white woman, and a white guy who lives with a black woman, and he keeps asking them if they'd all like to go down to Georgia with him for a vacation.

Ronnie used to be a professor of health at Michigan State, and I'm a nut about health, so we spent a lot of time sitting around talking about things like proper diet. I watch everything I eat. Starting in March, till I go to training camp four months later, I eliminate all sugar and salt from my diet. Fatty foods, forget it, and I won't touch anything that's fried. My body fat gets down to about 5 percent, and my blood count, my cholesterol level, they're better than a healthy teenager's.

I don't cheat on the diet, either. I think it was Dr. Haas, the eat-to-win doctor, who said the body can handle an occasional dietary indiscretion, but the mind can't handle the guilt, and that's the way I feel.

I started the diet in 1985, living in Pensacola during the off-season, and after three months of it, I decided to celebrate by going with Kit to my favorite Southern fried chicken place in the world. They gave me three pieces of the chicken, and I could only eat one, and I didn't feel good, and when I got home, I could actually feel the grease rolling around in my stomach. It was horrible.

I need every little edge I can get. The difference between winning the 100-meter dash in the Olympics and coming in fourth and not even getting a medal is the snap of a finger, that's all. I keep that in mind all the time. I think of that at night, and if I want a snack, you know what I have? Cereal with fruit in it—that's my dessert.

Ronnie and I tried to keep the fact I was living in his place secret for a while because the Giants, like most organizations, believe in segregation—between management and players. Ronnie's actually part of management, and I hope I'm actually a player.

Of course, guys found out about it and started kidding Ronnie, who used to be good friends with John Mistler, that now he had a new pet white receiver.

■ If the New York Giants seemed to be stumbling offensively in the early weeks of the 1985 season, if Phil Simms seemed to be struggling to match his brilliance of 1984, there was good reason. Simms was surrounded by strangers.

Kevin Belcher, the starting center in 1984, was gone, the victim of a midwinter automobile accident that destroyed his career.

Earnest Gray, a starting wide receiver, the Giants' most dangerous pass-catcher for six years, was gone, sitting out the season in a salary dispute that would finish his career.

Zeke Mowatt, the starting tight end, on the brink of stardom, was gone, his knee ripped up so badly in the final exhibition game against Pittsburgh that he had to undergo surgery.

William Roberts, a starting tackle, was gone—he, too, recuperating from knee surgery, his damaged in training camp.

Rob Carpenter, a starting running back, a wise and solid veteran, was still around, but hobbled, his knee injured, like Mowatt's, against the Steelers.

A new lineup was taking shape.

A rookie from Notre Dame, Mark Bavaro, moved in at tight end.

Another rookie, George Adams, from Kentucky, became the second running back, behind Joe Morris, sharing playing time with newcomer Maurice Carthon, a magnificent blocker salvaged from the New York Generals of the dying United States Football League.

Bart Oates, another survivor of the USFL who was spotted and signed by George Young's staff, became the center, and Brad Benson, for the second year in a row, took Roberts's place at tackle.

Bobby Johnson replaced Gray.

(The rest of the team was transformed, too. Three All-Pros were missing: Cornerback Mark Haynes, All-NFL four years in a row, engaged in a bitter contract dispute; punter Dave Jennings, All-NFL five times, released after eleven seasons as a Giant; and place-kicker Ali Haji-Sheikh, All-NFL in his rookie season, his magic diminished in 1984, sidelined by a hamstring injury. All three were replaced by free agents, hungry and unknown, Parcells's kind of guys.)

In the third game of the 1985 season, Oates was promoted to the starting lineup, flanked by Billy Ard and Chris Godfrey at the guards, and Karl Nelson and Brad Benson at the tackles, the five men a unit for the first time. They started the next thirty-five games in a row—thirty regular-season games and five post-season—straight through Super Bowl XXI.

Parcells labeled his offensive line "The Suburbanites," an appropriate tribute to their off-season interests—Benson is a Jaguar dealer, Ard a stockbroker, Oates a law student, Godfrey a banker and Nelson an engineer—and to their wonderfully pronounceable and euphonious names, which rank them right up there with the front five of Merrill Lynch, Pierce, Fenner & Smith, or the front four of Batten, Barton, Durstine & Osborn.

"We're the kind of guys," Billy Ard said, "our mothers drove us to football practice."

But Parcells also called his five offensive linemen his "lunchpail guys," his "blue-collar workers," and if there seems to be a sizable difference between suburbanites and, say, sandhogs, it is the difference between Nelson, Benson, Ard, Oates & Godfrey off the field—and on. They are strikingly sweet and gentle men off the field. They are killers on. They protect Phil Simms with a fierceness that reflects their affection for him and their respect for his strength and courage.

Phil Simms is a "lunchpail" quarterback.

CONKS We started the 1985 season slowly. The defense looked good beating Philadelphia, 21–0. The whole team looked terrible losing to Green Bay, 23–20.

David Fishof hadn't finished negotiating my new contract yet, so I gave him some ammunition in the first few games. Against the Eagles, I returned the opening kickoff 46 yards to set up one touchdown, and then I returned a punt 37 yards to set up another. Against the Packers, I forced a fumble and recovered it, wrestling the ball away from Walter Stanley on a kickoff return.

Then we played St. Louis, which had won its first two. The game was at Giants Stadium, and in the third quarter, we had a 13–10 lead and the ball on the Cardinals' 20-yard line.

Simms called the play: "Half right seventy-four double seam." I was on the left side. I had an option. I was supposed to run straight down the field or, if I saw there was nobody in the middle, I was supposed to run a post pattern, cut diagonally across the field.

Nobody was in the middle. I ran a post. Leonard Smith of

St. Louis was playing bump-and-run, up tight on me. I threw my head to the outside, because I'd run an "out" on him earlier, and he kind of took the fake. I cut to the inside. Simms spotted me. I was wide open, heading toward the end zone.

SIMMS He was well covered. I just stuck it in there.

CONKS The pass was perfect. I didn't have to dive for it or juggle it or anything. I caught a touchdown pass for the first time in my professional career.

Simms to McConkey.

Six points.

SIMMS Conks made a weak-ass-looking spike. He didn't know what to do, he was so surprised he scored. When we watched the films a couple of days later, he caught hell from everybody. "Damn, McConkey, that's a terrible spike."

It was like a singles hitter hitting a home run. He didn't know how to trot around the bases.

CONKS Simms and I decided that if I was so bad at spiking, then someday, when he threw me a touchdown pass, I'd throw the ball right back to him and let him spike it.

We've talked about that for two years now, and we've never done it. Of course, we haven't had all that many opportunities.

The next time I caught a touchdown pass at Giants Stadium was in 1987, in the playoffs, against San Francisco. We couldn't do it then because, when I caught the ball, Simms was lying flat on the field.

He knew from the roar of the crowd that I hadn't dropped it.

SIMMS I overthrew Bobby Johnson in practice a few days after the St. Louis game.

"Are we ever gonna complete a pass around here?" Parcells inquired.

I threw behind Lionel Manuel.

"Simms," Parcells said, "I hope we can complete some today because I need some sleep. I didn't sleep last night."

Conks dropped one.

"Are you gonna complete some passes today, or am I gonna go home and worry all night?"

Then he remembered his quarterbacking days in high school. "Two for seven," Parcells said. "I went two for seven with one interception, and then the coach said to me, 'Son, you're one of the reasons we're gonna run the ball all the time.' "

You never have to wonder what Parcells is thinking. He's as honest with us as a coach can be. He'll show displeasure with me or with anyone else. He'll needle me. He'll yell at me. He'll needle Lawrence Taylor. He won't yell at Lawrence. L.T. doesn't do anything bad enough to be yelled at.

CONKS We played Philadelphia twice in our first four games, and the week before the second Eagles game the weather was foul, and so was Parcells's mood. A storm whipped through New York, cutting into his practice time, and the day before the game, which is usually just a quick walk-through day, we still had a little serious work to do.

I was out early, fielding punts, not with a whole lot of success. I hadn't really loosened up, I had the sun in my eyes and a stiff wind was blowing. None of that bothered Parcells. "Sprint to it," he shouted. "Set your feet. Don't drift." His usual advice.

I couldn't even see the ball. Two punts fell in front of me, and Parcells went nuts. He went berserk. He was mad at the storm, and he took it out on me, yelling and screaming, "Catch the damned ball!"

I blew up. "How the hell you expect me to get to the ball?"

I yelled back. "I haven't stretched. Nobody's stretched. The sun's in my eyes. You try catching the damned ball."

He hollered louder, and the guys started mimicking him. "Catch the freakin' ball, McConkey," they shouted. "Catch the freakin' ball."

I was so pissed I started sprinting after the punts. I went all out. I ran. I stretched. I dove. I caught everything and I just whipped the ball downfield and I didn't even look at Parcells. I wouldn't give him the satisfaction.

Then I felt something in my hamstring. I finished the practice and went into the training room and got some ice on it, and Parcells walked in and said, "What did you do?" And I said, "I pulled my hamstring—shaggin' punts."

It wasn't all that bad, but I wanted him to worry. Let him feel a little guilt for a change. The next day, game day, the hamstring was fine, and I got to the locker room early, and Parcells was already there, drinking his coffee.

He looked at me. "You were mad at me yesterday, weren't you?" he said.

"Yeah," I said, "and I get mad at my father sometimes, too."

I knew he couldn't help it. He's got to yell at me. He's got to keep my fire lit.

SIMMS We had a 10–3 lead over Philadelphia with just three minutes to play when I went to pass from my own end zone. One of the Eagles reached up and batted the ball out of my hand and into the hands of a Philadelphia cornerback, Herman Edwards, who just had to take a couple of steps over the goal line for a touchdown that tied up the game.

The last time I'd seen Herman Edwards score a touchdown was on television. I was a senior at Morehead State, and I was watching the Sunday night sports, and I saw The Fumble, the play when Joe Pisarcik tried to hand off and the ball got loose.

It was Herman Edwards who picked up the ball and ran for the touchdown that beat the Giants.

I remember seeing it and feeling sorry for Pisarcik.

Later, Joe and I became teammates, and he was a hell of a good guy, and that's what he ought to be remembered for, not The Fumble.

CONKS We beat the Eagles anyway, to improve our record to three and one, and the victory belonged to two guys in particular—Jim Burt, the nose tackle, and Elvis Patterson, the cornerback. Burt had a quarterback sack and seventeen tackles, and on the second play of overtime, Patterson intercepted a pass and ran 29 yards for a touchdown that ended the game.

I love both of them. They're my kind of football players. They have no right to be in the NFL, but they are. They came to the Giants as free agents, Burt from the University of Miami, Patterson from Kansas University.

Burt was from Buffalo, originally. His father was a truck-driver. I didn't know him back home—he was a couple of years behind me in school—but I knew what he had to be like. At Miami he played defensive tackle, and he got some All-American mention, but nobody drafted him because they thought he was too short. He said he was six-foot-one, but everybody knew he was lying. He was six foot, maybe.

All you have to know about Patterson is that he only weighed 180 pounds at Kansas, but he not only played cornerback, he filled in at linebacker and defensive end. In the Big Eight—against teams like Oklahoma and Nebraska. Nobody drafted him either.

But George Young gave both of them a chance in mini-camp, Burt in 1981 and Patterson in 1984, and both fought and clawed their way into contracts that got them to training camp. Burt was a legend in his training camp. He had six or seven roommates who got cut, one after the other, and he was so afraid of being cut himself, he used to sleep under the bed, so that the coaches wouldn't be able to find him. Now he says that's not true, that he just hid under the covers, but either way he wasn't going to let them get rid of him. If a coach had tried, Burt probably would've decked him. He got into so many scuffles in training camp his nickname was "Sluggo." He wore thick-soled workboots so that he would look taller.

During his rookie season, Burt wanted to get into one game so badly he walked up behind Parcells, who was the defensive coordinator, and belted Bill with a forearm to the back to get his attention. He knocked Parcells onto the field, and Parcells started screaming at him and hasn't stopped since, but the next series of downs, Burt was on the field.

We call him Parcells's son, or Parcells, Jr., because he *is* Parcells, he really is. He's Parcells's favorite. "I've never met a guy that tough," Parcells once said. "You could do anything to him—drop him from a building, from an airplane, anything—and he'd show up to play. He's one of my parking-lot guys, the kind who would just nod their heads, pack their bags and be early if I told 'em we had a game in some shopping center parking lot, for no money, at six A.M. some Wednesday. He just loves it."

I like to think I'm like that, too. So is Elvis. Both he and Burt had to make their marks first on the special teams, the suicide teams. In his rookie season, Burt made twenty tackles covering kickoffs and punts. In his rookie season, Patterson made sixteen tackles covering kickoffs and punts, and blocked two field-goal attempts, one in the regular season and one in the playoffs.

Elvis takes his share of abuse from Parcells, too. Coach calls him "Toast" to remind him not to get burned by wide receivers. Parcells has nicknames for everybody. He calls Simms "Blondie." He used to call me "Weasel."

SIMMS I always did everything I could to help Jim Burt fit in. I even taught him how to play gin rummy, just as Brian Kelley had once taught me. But Burt never did show any gratitude. Finally, he dropped out of my classes. "Why am I trying to play you?" Burt said. "It's like beating my head against a rock. I mean, I feel like if I break even, I've done something."

The longer I was in the league, the less people were willing to play cards with me.

■ In the Giants' next two games, against Dallas and Cincinnati, Phil Simms passed for 945 yards. No one in the history of the NFL had ever gained so many yards passing in two consecutive games. The Giants scored 59 points against Dallas and Cincinnati—and lost both games.

Against Dallas, the Giants trailed at halftime, 14–6. In the third quarter, Simms sizzled. He threw three touchdown passes, 51 and 23 yards to Lionel Manuel, 70 yards to George Adams, and the Giants took a 26–14 lead.

Then Simms stumbled. He gave up an interception and fumbled twice, and the second fumble, in the closing minutes, set up Rafael Septien's third field goal of the fourth quarter, a field goal that lifted the Cowboys to a 30–29 victory.

Simms passed for 432 yards against Dallas, a personal record that lasted for only seven days.

SIMMS We went into Cincinnati with a simple game plan: We were going to run the ball down their throats. But the Bengals took the opening kickoff, drove for a touchdown, stopped our running game cold, scored again, shut us down again and, before we knew it, we were losing, 21–0. We had no choice but to throw the ball.

I threw. I threw great, better than I'd ever thrown in my life, better than I've ever thrown since. My arm was never more accurate, never stronger. It didn't make any difference if the receiver was covered, I'd still get the ball to him. I could fire it through the slightest opening. I couldn't do anything wrong.

One time, Lionel Manuel was running a real deep flag pattern, cutting to the outside, and before he even made his move —he was still leaning inside—I saw I was about to get hit, I dropped back, I jumped and I threw the ball, just let it go, no real idea whether Lionel was going to be anywhere near it or not. Then I got killed, but as I hit the ground, I heard this kind of groan from the Cincinnati crowd, and I knew Lionel had caught the ball. He'd caught the ball right in stride, a perfect pass, for about a 35-yard gain. I just said, "Damn, I'm hot!"

Lionel caught eight passes for more than 100 yards, and Mark Bavaro caught twelve, a record for the team, for almost 200. I hit nine different receivers—even McConkey had three catches—and I wound up completing forty of sixty-two passes for 513 yards. My attempts, my completions and my yardage all broke Giant records, two of Charlie Conerly's and one of Y. A. Tittle's. The only quarterback who'd ever passed for more yards in an NFL game was Norm Van Brocklin of the Los Angeles Rams, and that was before I was born.

Still, I made a couple of mistakes that, in the end, cost us the game. In the third quarter, we cut their lead to 21–20, and we had the ball again. I went back to pass, and they blitzed. Somebody came in free. Nobody touched him. I made a hell of a play to get away from him, straight-armed him and started sliding to my left. Then, off balance, I threw across the field to my right. I threw a perfect spiral, and I said to myself, "Damn, what a throw!" Just then—woof!—James Griffin cut in front of the receiver, intercepted and ran for a touchdown. I couldn't have thrown the ball any better. I just never saw Griffin.

A little later, I fumbled, setting up another Bengal touchdown. Cincinnati beat us, 35–30, even though we outgained them, 477 yards (I was sacked seven times) to 199. They actually had negative yardage in the second half, but, because of my mistakes, still managed to score those two decisive touchdowns.

Several reporters made it a point to mention in their stories that my interceptions and fumble had cost us the game, but when we watched the films, the coaches didn't get on me at all. Just the opposite. In the offensive team meeting, Ron Erhardt ran some of my passes back and forth and said, "Goddamn it, men, who else can make that play?" He didn't have to stick up for me in front of my teammates, but he did, and I was glad. I really kind of needed him to do that.

Parcells walked up to me at practice a few days later and, out of nowhere, said, "Hey, I made a stupid mistake in '83. If I knew then what I know now, I never would've made that decision." And he walked away.

I wanted to ask him how close he came to getting rid of me in 1983. I know he wanted to get rid of me. I just don't know how close he came.

That was the only time since 1983 he ever brought up his decision to bench me.

CONKS Parcells told us that if we didn't win seven of our last ten games, we could forget about getting in the playoffs. We heard him. We won our next four in a row, starting with a victory over Washington and ending with a victory over the Los Angeles Rams. During our winning streak, Joe Morris became a giant.

The first seven games of the season, Joe only scored three touchdowns and ran for 337 yards, not very impressive numbers. But in our last nine games, he scored eighteen touchdowns and ran for 999 yards.

Joe rushed for more than 100 yards in six of our last nine games. In his whole career, up till then, he had rushed for more than 100 yards only once.

His longest run in our first ten games was less than 20 yards. In our last six games, he scored touchdowns on runs of 65, 58, 56 and 41 yards. Suddenly, Joe Morris was a super-star.

Some people used to say that Joe was too small to play in the NFL, but Parcells always said, "Joe's not small. He's short."

At five-foot-seven, Joe's the only man on the team shorter than me. But there isn't anybody stronger than Joe. He's awesome in the weight room. He's got the strongest legs in the world. You couldn't add more musculature. I've seen linebackers shake their heads after tackling him. They can't believe anyone's so powerful.

SIMMS I was scared the day we played the Rams. I was intim-idated. I don't think I've ever been intimidated mentally, but I have been intimidated physically, and that was one of those days. I just didn't want to get hit. I didn't want to take a beating. I was hurting.

I'd hurt my knee the week before against Tampa Bay, and when I started warming up, it still hurt so bad I thought I was going to cry. I think Parcells could tell. He was pumping me before the game. "By God, Simms," he said, "there ain't many who can stand in there every week, but you can."

I played the whole game in fear, and nobody said anything, none of the coaches, none of the players. I didn't have a bad game, sixteen-for-thirty for 239 yards, including a 36-yard touchdown pass to Bobby Johnson that helped us come back from a 13–0 deficit. I also threw a couple of interceptions, but we beat the Rams, who were leading their division, and we improved our record to seven and three.

When I got home, I didn't eat much dinner, and I was real quiet. "Why are you so quiet?" my wife asked me.

"Oh, I just don't feel real good," I said.

"Are you disappointed in the way you played?" Diana asked.

"Well, yeah, a little."

"Phil, your heart just wasn't in it today," she said, "I could see that."

She didn't realize exactly what she was saying, but she was right. She was absolutely right. "Yeah, I was scared," I said. "I was scared to get hit."

She was the only one who knew it.

I was kind of glad I didn't have to face our defense on Sundays. Our defense did terrible things to quarterbacks. The second time we played the Redskins in 1985, L.T. had thirteen tackles, a fumble recovery and two sacks. On one of the sacks, Lawrence fell on Joe Theismann and broke his leg and ended his career.

The injury started Jay Schroeder's career. He came off the bench in the second quarter and passed for more than 200 yards and the winning touchdown. The Redskins beat us, 23–21. Still, with a record of seven and four, we were tied with Dallas for first place in our division.

The next week, against St. Louis, our defense zeroed in on Neil Lomax and his replacement, my old friend and rival, Scott Brunner. The result: eight sacks, three interceptions, no broken bones. George Martin, who comes as close to being a saint as anybody on our team, had three sacks, a fumble recovery and an interception that he ran back 56 yards for the sixth touchdown of his career. George is a *defensive* end, and he's scored more touchdowns than some offensive ends I know. We won easily and stayed tied with Dallas for first place.

After we blew a twelve-point lead in the last quarter and lost to Cleveland, 35–33, we beat Houston and had a nine-and-five record, the same as Dallas. We had a chance to clinch our division title if we could win our next game—if we could beat the Cowboys in Dallas. It had been twenty-two years since the Giants had finished first in anything.

Damn, we came close. I threw fifty passes, passed for more

than 300 yards and for two touchdowns, one to Bobby Johnson, one to Tony Galbreath, giving us a 14–7 lead in the second quarter. The Cowboys lost two quarterbacks, first Danny White with a shoulder injury, then Gary Hogeboom with a concussion.

But we lost the game. Two interceptions killed us. Ed "Too Tall" Jones reached up and batted one of my passes in the air, and Jim Jeffcoat grabbed the ball and ran it back 65 yards to tie the score at 14–14 in the second quarter. Then, in the last minute of the game, when we were losing, 28–21, we drove down to the Dallas 16-yard line, 16 yards from a touchdown that would've tied the score, and I got intercepted again.

It was our worst defeat of the year—by *seven* points. We'd lost six games—by a combined total of twenty points. We had been ahead in every game we'd played except one, the Cincinnati game, and we should have won that one.

We knew we could beat anybody.

CONKS We should've beat Dallas. We should've put them away early. It was my fault. The first time we had the ball, I put a great move on Everson Walls, maybe the best move of my life, and I was wide open for a touchdown, not a Cowboy near me. Simms threw, and I thought I was going to have to dive for the ball, and I twisted my body, and by the time I realized I didn't have to dive—it was a perfect throw—my body was out of control. I dropped the ball.

I don't drop passes. I look them in. I fold my arms over the ball. I hang on. But I dropped that one. I never forgot it. Parcells didn't either. "My wife Judy could've caught that one," he needled me more than a year later.

Simms never said anything. He knew I didn't *want* to drop the ball. He's great like that. He understands that receivers make mistakes. He kept throwing to me, and I caught six passes for 128 yards, the best day of my career—statistically. But for once, the statistics didn't mean a thing.

Dallas clinched the division title.

We had to win our final game to make sure we got into the playoffs as a wild-card team.

SIMMS This time, our last game of the regular season meant something—meant *everything*—and we played as if it did. We took a 28–3 lead over Pittsburgh by halftime, then coasted to a 28–10 victory. I didn't throw much. I didn't have to. Most of the time, I just handed the ball to Joe Morris, and he ran for 202 yards and three touchdowns, the best day of his career.

If we'd lost to Pittsburgh, we would've been eliminated. But our victory put us into the playoffs, and for the wild-card game against San Francisco, the defending Super Bowl champions, we even had the home-field advantage.

The Giants hadn't played a post-season game at home since 1962.

I found out what Tittle and Gifford and Huff must've felt like. When we came out of the tunnel at Giants Stadium, the crowd greeted us with the loudest roar I'd ever heard. I knew there was no way we were going to lose.

Jim Burt sacked Joe Montana twice. Our defense held Roger Craig, their best runner, to 23 yards rushing. I threw touchdown passes to both of our tight ends, Mark Bavaro and Don Hasselbeck. We knocked San Francisco's Super Bowl champions out of the playoffs, 17–3.

They'd knocked us out in 1984 and 1981.

I guess we won another little one.

CONKS Elvis Patterson and Kenny Hill both got hurt against San Francisco, and if one more defensive back had gone down, either Andy Headen, the linebacker, or I would have had to go in. I hadn't played defense since high school, except for a few plays in the Japan Bowl. Just in case, Parcells had me practice a little at safety before our second playoff game, against the Bears in Chicago. The Bears had lost only one game all season.

GATORADE ®

1986–1987

■ They had paid their dues, the New York Giants of Simms and Taylor and Morris and Parcells, they had paid in blood and sweat, and now they were ready, if not for champagne, which is banned from championship locker rooms in the NFL, at least for Gatorade.

Not many people realized how close the Giants had come to being a dominating team in 1985, how thin the line had been between the good 10–6 season they enjoyed and a great 13–3 or 14–2 or even 15–1 season. An extra fourteen points, judiciously distributed, and the Giants would have been 15–1 in the regular season, matching the glittering record of the Chicago Bears.

The team was in place, especially on offense, so carefully and finely constructed that the Giants' first six draft selections in 1986 were all defensive players. An all-veteran starting lineup was set on defense, too, thin in the line and in the secondary, but deep and devastating at linebacker.

The 1986 Giants had everything going for them—talent, experience and, not least, hunger. Only one man who won a place on the roster, defensive back Kenny Hill, had ever played in a Super Bowl; for the rest, it was still only a dream.

Phil Simms was ready. He had started thirty-six straight games in 1984 and 1985. Phil McConkey was ready, too, ready to face one of those uphill struggles that seemed to come as natural to him as breathing.

The rules of the NFL in 1986 permitted the Giants only forty-five active players, not the forty-nine they had been allowed during McConkey's rookie season. The Giants had carried five wide receivers in 1984 and 1985, but in 1986, they might limit themselves to four.

They might not have room for McConkey.

1986

In which Simms makes his Pro Bowl
debut, and McConkey makes his
comeback

SIMMS We saved our worst game of the year for last. We
didn't do anything right in Chicago. I completed only three
passes to my wideouts, Joe Morris ran for only 32 yards and
Sean Landeta, who'd become a great punter for us, made the
worst punt of his life. Kicking from the end zone, he stepped
forward and dropped the ball, and a gust of wind caught it.
When he brought his kicking leg up, he barely grazed the ball.
It bounced a couple of yards, and one of the Bears picked it
up, took a few steps and was in the end zone. That was the
only score of the first half, but in the second, Jim McMahon
threw two touchdown passes, and they won, 21–0. Three
weeks later, the Bears won the Super Bowl, which meant that
for the fourth time in six years, we'd ended our season against
the team that won the championship.

CONKS I made a great catch in the closing minutes against the
Bears, going up in traffic and taking big hits from Gary Fencik
and—I think—Mike Singletary, who *are* big hitters, and hold-

ing on to the ball. The catch brought us inside their 5-yard line, threatening their shutout.

I lined up in the slot, with a defensive back over me, and the Bears began barking like dogs, taunting us. They expected a pass play. Instead, we called a draw, and normally, on a draw, I'll just run a pattern and let the defensive back follow me. But this time I was so frustrated and angry I cut him, and he fell on top of me and grabbed my face mask and started twisting my neck. I was bucking back and forth, trying to bounce him off me. George Adams finally came and pulled the guy off, and I wanted a fight. I began leaping over people trying to get at the guy who'd twisted my neck. I swung at everybody. "What are you trying to do?" the referee shouted at me. "Start a riot?"

I was hyperventilating in the locker room after the game.

Our Super Bowl season actually started in that locker room in Chicago in January. Coach Parcells told us after our defeat he would do anything and everything he could to get to the next level. He expected us to, too. He told us George Martin and Harry Carson didn't deserve what had happened. He said George and Harry deserved to be champions. He had us aiming at Super Bowl XXI before they even played Super Bowl XX.

Our Super Bowl season almost ended a few hours later. We lost an engine on our DC-10 on the way back from Chicago. I heard it go dead. The pilot came on the speaker and said there was no problem, but I knew better. I could hear him trying to restart the engine, and he couldn't.

When we approached Newark Airport, we got a tremendous reception—not from fans, from the crash crew, ambulances and fire engines lining the runway, lights flashing, the standard emergency procedures.

For a while, I wondered if I was ever going to get a chance to make a diving catch for a touchdown in the Super Bowl.

But we made it down okay.

SIMMS My son, Christopher, told me he was glad we lost to Chicago. "Why?" I said, and he said, "Well, I like the Bears, Daddy, and, besides, now I've got you home to play with me."

Christopher had me at home for a few weeks, and then I went off to Hawaii to play in the Pro Bowl, for the first time in my career. When I met Randy White of the Cowboys, who was one of my NFC teammates, I was shocked: He actually seemed to be a nice guy.

I'd never met him before, except on the field, and on the field, Randy is just plain mean. Once, as I completed a pass, he charged into me, drove right through my chest, then kind of held me up as I kept running backward. I couldn't stop and I couldn't fall down until Randy decided we were both going to fall down.

When he did, we tumbled, and he dug the top of his helmet into my chin and ripped it open. I was lying there bleeding and groaning, not saying a word, just groaning, not even loud, and he looked over at me and said, "Aw, shut up!" He killed me and then he told me to shut up. And I did.

When we met in Hawaii, I was almost afraid to talk to him, he's so intimidating. I was definitely afraid to shake hands with him. I thought he'd crush my hand. But he couldn't have been nicer.

Randy White's mystique is like Lawrence's. They are intimidators. But I'm not afraid of Lawrence.

"Oh, nice hit, Lawrence," I've said to him. "Why don't you take your skirt off?"

Of course, I've said that to him on the golf course, never on the football field.

I had a pretty good game in the Pro Bowl. I wasn't supposed to start, but with Jim McMahon still recovering from New Orleans, I got to play almost the whole game. The American Conference was leading at halftime, 24–7, but in the second half I threw three touchdown passes for the National Conference, the last one with less than three minutes to go in the game. We won, 28–24, and I was named the Most Valuable Player.

I enjoyed it. It was fun having Walter Payton for a running back, James Lofton for a pass receiver and Jim Covert for a blocker. It made it easier to face my old friends Mark Gastineau and Joe Klecko on the opposite side of the line.

CONKS I'd always dreamed of being a superstar, and in 1986, finally, thanks to David Fishof, I became one. He got me into "The Superstars" competition, and one morning, at breakfast, while I was sitting with one real superstar, Bernie Kosar, the Cleveland quarterback, four more superstars were sitting at the next table: Herschel Walker, Renaldo Nehemiah, Willie Gault and James Lofton, all world-class track-and-field athletes before they played in the NFL.

Willie Gault told me later that they were arguing about who was the best athlete in the room.

"I'll tell you who the best athlete in this room is," Walker said. "The best athlete's sitting over there." And Herschel pointed at me.

"What do you mean?" Willie Gault said.

"Can you imagine not playing football for five years, not competing in any sports at all," Herschel said, "and then coming back and making an NFL team? That's what he did."

Nobody argued with him.

That may have been the best compliment I've ever received.

SIMMS I was sitting in David Fishof's office not long after the Pro Bowl when Jim Burt called. "Hey, tell Burt I've been traded to the Rams," I told David.

"You hear about Simms?" Fishof said.

"What's that?" Burt said.

"They traded him. He's going to the Rams. They're getting two first-round draft choices, and a couple of players."

"You're shitting me," Burt said.

"No," David said. "But don't say anything. It won't be announced for a few days."

Burt was furious. The next day, he went to the stadium and marched into Parcells's office and said, "You guys have got to be the dumbest sons of bitches in the whole world. Get rid of me. I don't want to play here any more. You're getting rid of Simms, you get rid of me, too."

Parcells looked at him. "What the hell are you talking about, Burt?" he said.

"You know what the hell I'm talking about," Burt said.

It must've taken Parcells five minutes to calm Burt down and convince him that I wasn't being traded.

Burt wanted to kill Fishof and me.

CONKS I knew something was bothering L.T. in 1985, that he didn't have his usual energy, especially not late in the season, but I didn't know it was drugs, not till he admitted he was undergoing substance-abuse treatment.

It just wasn't like L.T. to be tired. Normally he's got about the same energy level as I do, only he's got the body to go with it. I knew he had a new baby, and I just thought maybe the baby was keeping him up at night.

I don't know enough about cocaine or anything like that to recognize the symptoms. I've never been around the stuff. I get high on diving catches. I get high on pretty dates. I even get high on interviews.

I don't think anybody'll ever be able to convince the Washington Redskins that L.T. wasn't L.T. in 1985. In our two games against them, he had twenty-six tackles, four sacks and one fumble recovery, one-fourth of his tackles for the whole season, more than one-fourth of his sacks and one-half of his fumble recoveries. He broke Joe Theismann's leg on one sack, a clean hit that ended the quarterback's career.

Every team fears Lawrence Taylor, but the Redskins, understandably, fear him the most. We once picked up a running back who'd been cut by Washington, and he told us that even in their training camp all they talked about was L.T. and how they were going to stop him. They knew that on any one play, he could destroy their team.

The strange thing is, L.T. doesn't train very hard. He won't even come into the weight room. His idea of lifting weights is carrying his golf clubs to the first tee. It's scary to think what he would be like if he trained like us mere mortals.

When "The Superstars" competition appeared on TV, Byron Williams called up Tony Galbreath and, in his fast, high-pitched voice, said, "How'd that little mother get in there? What did he ever do to be a superstar?"

Byron was laughing, but he had a point. I certainly wasn't in the same class with sprinters like Herschel Walker, Willie Gault, Renaldo Nehemiah and the baseball player, Vince Coleman, not for 100 yards. But Herschel gave me some tips on getting out of the blocks, and for about 40 yards, I was able to keep up with Willie Gault.

After 40 yards, I got to know the sight of his elbows and his rear end better than anybody in the world.

SIMMS I choked. The pressure got to me. I thought I was going to break par for the first time in my life. I was three under with three holes to play, and I threw up all the way in. Unbelievable! Three straight bogies. Had to sink a four-foot putt on the eighteenth for my bogey. Gave me a 72. Even par. Still the best round of my life. I play to an 8-handicap.

I was playing at Knickerbocker, the club I belong to, in my regular threesome, with Larry Feroli and Artie Odabash. We're like The Three Stooges. We always play together. We get together with our families, too, go out to dinner all the time.

Larry's in the food business, and Artie's in real estate. They're both maybe twenty years older than me, but they act like they think they're in their midtwenties. We're easy to spot on the course. Larry shaves his head.

I met Artie through Father Moore, our team priest. Artie's an incredible Giant fan, and he just lives and dies with me. "I'll be glad when you retire," he tells me, "so I can go back to enjoying these games."

CONKS Simms wanted to do some throwing in June, so I came up from Pensacola, and Bavaro came down from Boston, and the three of us worked out for a few days. Bavaro was running around without a shirt on, and I turned to Simms and said, "You know, that's the best body I've ever seen—on a guy."

Simms was impressed, too. He needles everybody, but he doesn't needle Bavaro. Nobody does.

When Mark was a rookie, at the end of training camp, Lamar Leachman came up to him one day and said, "You're some kind of a football player, kid, you're gonna be a great football player, you got it all, kid, and you got a great nickname. Rambo. That's a great nickname, you like the nickname, kid?"

And Bavaro, who's very religious and very soft-spoken and never swears, said to Lamar, "I'd like to kill the mother who gave it to me."

After Bavaro went home, Simms and I flew down to Kentucky to participate in George Adams's football camp. George was awesome as a rookie in 1985. He had the potential to be one of the great running backs in the NFL. I could feel the excitement building, the bond building among the players. I knew that 1986 was going to be our year, and I knew that Simms and Bavaro and Adams were going to be big parts of it. I was going to be a part of it, too.

* * *

The first week of training camp, with eleven wide receivers on the roster, Pat Hodgson called the five veterans together —Lionel, Bobby, Stacy, Byron and me—and told us, "We can get the job done with just the guys who've been here, just you five. We don't need anybody else."

I appreciated the reassurance.

Still, I remembered what Pat had told us when I was a rookie: "I'm not married to the veterans."

Three of our rookie wideouts—Vince Warren, Ron Brown and Solomon Miller—were drafted in the first six rounds. All three ran the forty in four-point-three.

Parcells kept making cracks in meetings about the guys who just want to impress the girls, and then he'd look at me and at Conrad Goode, a six-foot-six 285-pound blonde who could impress the girls just by breathing.

I thought Parcells was being unfair.

I probably went out less than any other straight bachelor in football.

I thought I had a great training camp. I concentrated on polishing my receiving skills. I ran good patterns. I found the seams in the zones. I beat guys. I caught the ball. I was more relaxed than I had ever been before. Parcells hated seeing me relaxed. He wanted me to be on edge, scared, pissed off. He wanted me starting fights.

In 1984, I got in a fight with Elvis Patterson. We were both rookies, free agents, scrambling for jobs. I thought he was holding me too much. He thought I was holding him too much. He pushed me on one play, and I threw the ball at him, and we went at it. Nothing serious, just a pushing and shoving thing, but Parcells loved it. He loved our free-agent mentality, our scratching, clawing blue-collar outlook.

In 1985, I got in a fight with Herb Welch. I was going through my usual bad time sleeping, and I was tired and pissed off at everything, and I thought he hit me too hard one time, and up went my fists, and I just began flailing away. Welch looked at me like I was crazy. He didn't want any part of it. He was right. I was crazy. And Parcells loved it.

In 1986, I didn't have a fight.

"C'mon, McConkey," Parcells yelled. "You got to get going."

They showed up at one of the Wednesday night barbecues at training camp—no meetings on Wednesday nights—and they were dressed to kill: my date, Renee, and her friend, Conrad Goode's fiancée, both of them with knockout bodies. They weren't supposed to arrive until after the barbecue. Naturally, they attracted a little attention. I told them to wait for us with Simms's "date." His date was David Fishof.

Of course, Simms came over to check them out.

I think he approved.

SIMMS She was strong.

McConkey was out of his league.

Again.

Ron Erhardt and Pat Hodgson asked the quarterbacks to rate the wide receivers, and, as far as I know, all of us, me and Jeff Rutledge and Jeff Hostetler, ranked McConkey among the top three or four. The coaches listen to what we say, but, of course, we're not the final word.

CONKS I knew it would be Stacy Robinson or me. One of us was going to go. I certainly had more experience—Stacy was out with a broken hand most of 1985, his rookie season—but he was young and fast and promising. He was a sprint champion in high school and in college, and he was the Most Valuable Player in the Senior Bowl. He was a good receiver. He was a good football player.

We played our final exhibition game against Pittsburgh—
we beat them to wind up undefeated, and I scored a touchdown on a short pass from Jeff Hostetler—but after the game
I wondered if I was stripping off my Giant uniform for the last
time. I stared at the uniform for a long time.

I spent the next day at home, and, usually, Ronnie
Barnes has a pretty good inkling of who's coming and who's
going. But he didn't know anything. I don't think the
coaches had made up their minds yet. It was coming down
to the wire, a lot of debate, a lot of thought. With the forty-
five-player limit, we were only going to carry four wide
receivers.

Ironically, Stacy and I arrived at Giants Stadium at the
same time the following morning, and when we pulled up in
the parking lot, I kind of waited, read the paper for a little
while, let him go in first. I was really nervous.

Finally, I got out of my car, and, as I did, Simms pulled up,
and I waited for him, and we walked in together, through the
gate, down the hill, into the tunnel, talking but not saying
much. I saw Mike Sweatman, the special-teams assistant,
standing outside the locker room door.

It felt like we were walking in slow motion. I didn't want to
look at Mike. I didn't want to look at the door. I kept looking
at Simms, talking to him, and then I took a deep breath and
said, "Well, here we go," and as we turned toward the locker
room, Sweatman tapped me and said, "Phil, Coach wants to
see you upstairs. Whitey'll take you up." Whitey Wagner is
the locker room manager.

I knew then.

I knew I was no longer a New York Giant.

It was almost a relief. The pressure was off.

I went upstairs and sat down with Parcells, and he told me,
straight off, they were putting me on waivers, it was strictly a
numbers thing, he had to make a cut, and he didn't think I'd
done as well in training camp as he had expected. "I didn't
think you were yourself," he said. "If you didn't have your

number on your jersey, I wouldn't have thought it was you at camp."

I disagreed with him, of course. I told him I thought I had the best camp I ever had. I told him I thought he was wrong, he was making a mistake. I believed what I said, but I knew, and he knew, that he wasn't going to change his mind.

I went downstairs from Parcells's office, and I saw Pat Hodgson, and he had tears in his eyes, and he told me that cutting me was one of the hardest things he was ever part of. "I'm not gonna say goodbye," he said, " 'cause I'm gonna see you again. You know, you're going to be back."

I believed him. I really did. I felt that something very good was going to happen to the New York Giants, and that somehow I was going to be part of it.

Seven rookies made the team. Conrad Goode got cut, too.

SIMMS I wasn't just disappointed when I heard that Conks had been cut. I was very disappointed. I knew I was going to miss him—and I was pretty sure the team would, too.

CONKS Ronnie Barnes called me from the stadium the next morning and told me that Parcells wanted to speak to me. Parcells got on and said, "The Green Bay Packers just claimed you. They've been using Eddie Lee Ivery as their fourth wideout, and he's hurt, and they claimed you."

"Great," I said.

Parcells told me who to call in Green Bay.

"No matter what happens," I told him, "I think I should have made your team. I can contribute, and of course I think I'm better than the next guy. But I'll never have any bitter feelings. I appreciate what you've done for me. You gave me an opportunity as a twenty-six, twenty-seven-year-old to go ahead and play football. You gave me a chance when other teams would never even have looked at me. For that, I'll be forever grateful. You helped make a dream come true."

Parcells got kind of choked up. He told me he appreciated what I'd said, and he was sorry it didn't work out the way we'd hoped, and he wished me luck.

I said goodbye, and I got off the phone and I let out a yell, and I started running around the empty house, waving my arms like I was waving a towel, shouting, "I'm gonna be a Green Bay Packer, I'm gonna be a Green Bay Packer!"

All I could think of was all the great teams they'd had, and all the great players, Starr and Hornung and Taylor and Nitschke and Davis, and the whole Lombardi legend. I didn't care what their record was the last couple of years, or what their outlook was this year, they were the Green Bay Packers, and I was going to be a part of them.

I flew out to Green Bay that afternoon.

■ The day the 1986 NFL season began, the New York Giants were in trouble. They didn't have a running back. Joe Morris, their leading rusher in 1985, was seeking to renegotiate his contract. George Adams, their second leading rusher, was nursing a chipped bone in his pelvis. Rob Carpenter, their third leading rusher, was with the Los Angeles Rams, hoping to play out his tenth season as a professional. Ironically, Carpenter had left the Giants because he felt they had too many running backs.

Fortunately for the Giants, the day the 1986 NFL season began, they didn't have to play. They opened the next night, in Dallas, and a few hours before the game, Joe Morris agreed to a four-year contract that made him, at more than $500,000 a year, the highest-paid five-foot-seven in football.

The Cowboys' Herschel Walker, taller and higher-paid, made his NFL debut against the Giants. Walker ran for two touchdowns, and his second, with less than two minutes to play, gave Dallas a 31–28 victory. The Giants lost despite one of Phil Simms's "pretty good" games—he passed for 300 yards and three touchdowns—and a surprisingly good game for Morris.

Even though he had missed most of training camp and the exhibition season, Morris was the game's leading rusher—with 87 yards, only two fewer than Walker and his teammate, Tony Dorsett, gained combined.

The Giants had a running back.

But they didn't have a place-kicker, not one they could depend upon.

Thirty-four-year old Bob Thomas, discarded in 1985 by the Chicago Bears, attempted a 36-yard field goal for the Giants —and missed.

SIMMS Joe Montana suffered a ruptured disc in San Francisco's opening game and had to be operated on. Nobody expected him to play again in 1986. A lot of people thought his career was over. I hoped it wasn't.

I don't like some things Montana's said about me—he once told a reporter with a tape recorder that he thought I was too cocky—but that doesn't mean I want to see him get hurt. I don't want to see anybody get hurt, because I know what it's like, and it's miserable.

But even if he never played another game, at least Montana had the satisfaction of playing in two Super Bowls and winning two Super Bowls. He didn't have anything he still had to prove.

In our second game, we beat San Diego, 20–7, at Giants Stadium. Our defense was awesome—Terry Kinard and Kenny Hill had two interceptions apiece—and I played pretty good. For the second week in a row, I threw for 300 yards. But I got sacked four times, making it seven in two games, and after one of the sacks, Brad Benson whispered to me, "You come out of the pocket a little bit on that one?"

I hadn't moved an inch.

"Yeah," I said. "Yeah, I did."

"I thought so," Brad said. " 'Cause I had him. I had him as long as you stayed in the pocket."

You say anything to appease your linemen during the game.

At the end, Parcells got a Gatorade shower from Harry Carson and a big hug from Lawrence Taylor.

Parcells got sixteen more showers before the season was over. I don't know how many hugs he got.

The San Diego game was just a routine game, if you weren't playing quarterback in it. If you were, it was brutal. I stayed sore for more than three weeks afterward. I was in the training room every day, telling Ronnie Barnes, "Give me a rubdown, give me a whirlpool." I didn't bitch and moan in the locker room—I wouldn't get any sympathy there—but I did at home.

I couldn't ask for better receivers than Lionel Manuel and Mark Bavaro. In our third game, against the Raiders in Los Angeles, I completed six passes to each of them, and Lionel scored both our touchdowns, the second, the one that won the game, on a pass that was deflected by the Raiders.

Our kicking game was still in trouble. We waived Bob Thomas after one game, then picked up Joe Cooper, who, in two games, kicked two short field goals, from 20 yards and 21, but missed two from 39 and 43.

For our fourth game, we signed a new kicker, Raul Allegre, a Mexican who went to high school in the state of Washington, then college in Texas. He used to be with the Indianapolis Colts. We almost signed him after our opening game, but his agent wanted him to get a bonus for each extra point and for each field goal, and when the negotiations bogged down, Parcells sent Allegre packing.

He was working as a civil engineer in Indianapolis.

CONKS The first three weeks I spent in Green Bay, I didn't catch a pass, I didn't return a punt or a kickoff, I didn't go out on a date and we didn't win a game. We had a moral victory in our third game: We *almost* beat the Chicago Bears.

I played only on the kickoff team, trying to make a few tackles. On offense, I was behind James Lofton, Walter Stanley and Philip Epps, the wideouts who were the strength of the Packers. "Man, we got the best wide receivers in all football," I told them when I arrived, which was meant to be respectful, not cocky.

I'd played on two winning teams in New York, and I tried to get the Packers to think like winners. I waved my towel, cheered and hollered, but I didn't have much luck getting through to them. They'd been through such turmoil, a huge turnover in personnel and assistant coaches, and even their head coach, Forrest Gregg, the Hall of Fame tackle—he looked bigger than life to me—seemed to have trouble getting through to them.

He told the team before the first game, "There's more talent here than on any other team I've ever coached," but all the guys knew he took Cincinnati to the Super Bowl, with Ken Anderson and Chris Collinsworth, and so there went his credibility. Then he was so upset by the opening loss to Houston, he bitched about it for a whole week while we were getting ready to play New Orleans.

Aside from the football, I loved it in Green Bay. I lived in a hotel the first week, then moved into a cottage on a lake less than twenty miles from town. The other guys on the team thought I was insane, living that far away from the stadium, but it was a lovely place and it was a beautiful twenty-five-minute drive with no traffic and only a few deer. After driving the Jersey Turnpike every day, the road to Green Bay was nothing.

I loved being surrounded by the Lombardiisms that I'd lived by all my life: *The glory is not in never falling, but in rising every time you fall. You never achieve perfection, but if you seek it, you will achieve excellence. The harder you work, the harder it is to surrender.*

I watched the Giants on "Monday Night Football" and I followed them in the papers and I still thought of them as "we." I was wearing the Green Bay green-and-gold, but it was hard to think of myself as a Packer.

I didn't do much at night. I went over to Vince Ferragamo's house a few times—he's another one of Fishof's clients—to have dinner and play with his children, his three daughters. I brought the girls candy each time I went over. They wanted me to come to dinner every night. I also spent some time with Tom Flynn and his wife, Chris. Tom was a defensive back who went to Pitt.

I didn't meet one woman who interested me. You know, being around New York and all the beautiful women there, you get kind of spoiled. And having sex with somebody you don't care about is just a very temporary high. In the morning, you usually feel lousy about it. That's what I've heard anyway.

Besides, these days, with all the diseases that are going around, herpes and AIDS and who knows what else, it's just not worth it. I guess it's worth it to some guys. But not to me. I want to have a nice healthy family some day.

I got a lot of sleep in Green Bay.

SIMMS Against New Orleans, we fell behind for the third time in four games, spotted the Saints a 17–0 lead, then came back to win, 20–17. Raul Allegre tried two field goals, both from less than 30 yards, and made them both. Bavaro, who got his jaw broken and two teeth knocked out, caught seven passes, giving him twenty-five in four games, the most receptions in the conference.

But it was an expensive victory. Lionel Manuel sprained his left knee, and Mark Collins, our best kick returner, lost his helmet on one runback and suffered a concussion. Tony Galbreath had to return punts after Collins got hurt, which Tony hadn't done in years, and he fumbled two of the four punts he fielded.

With a three-game winning streak, and a chance for a strong

season, we needed a pass receiver who knew our routes and we needed someone who could return kicks.

In other words, we needed McConkey.

Besides, Christopher kept asking for him.

CONKS I was changing my shoes to go running after watching the films of the Minnesota game, our fourth straight defeat. "Hey, McConkey," Burt Gustafson, who works in the front office, called to me, "Coach Gregg wants to see you." I knew Eddie Lee Ivery was coming off the injured reserve list. I knew something had to give, and I figured the something was me. I figured I was getting cut again.

My feelings must have showed on my face, because Gustafson looked at me and said, "Don't worry, you've got a job."

I didn't know what he meant. I'd been practicing hard. I'd been lifting weights after everyone else left. I'd been studying films. I'd been running on my own. If I wasn't getting cut, what had I done wrong?

I walked into Coach Gregg's office, and he wasn't there. I sat down and waited. Then he walked in with a big smile on his face. "Got some good news for you," he said. "We just traded your rights back to the New York Giants."

It felt like it was Christmas morning, and Gregg was Santa Claus. I was ecstatic. I went to a pay phone and called my father and told him, and then I got a call from Parcells. He didn't know they had already told me. I think he wanted to break the news himself.

I don't blame him. Cutting players is one of the toughest things coaches have to do, and you don't very often get a chance to welcome one back. "When you get back here," Parcells told me, "you're going to play your ass off."

"Don't worry about that," I said. "I'll be there tonight."

"Hey, you got two days," he said. "We don't practice tomorrow. Just be here Wednesday."

The last thing I said to him was, "The grass is greener—
my ass!" That's one of his favorite expressions—*my ass*—
which is why I used it, and he loved it. "The grass is greener
—my ass!" He told me I was going to have to write it on the
bulletin board.

He also told me that the Packers drove a tough deal. "We
had to give up a blocking dummy and a couple of clipboards
for you," Parcells said.

SIMMS I came in to work out and I walked up to Ron Erhardt
and I said, "We got to get McConkey—"

And before I could finish, Ron said, "We got him. We made
a trade for him this morning."

Damn, I was glad. I missed him. I couldn't wait to start
picking on him again.

CONKS Ronnie Barnes met me at the airport, told me I had a
place to live, then drove me right to Giants Stadium. There
weren't any players around—it was their day off—but, of
course, the coaches were waiting.

Pat Hodgson gave me a big greeting, reminded me that he
knew I'd be back and asked me if, playing with Lofton and
Stanley and Epps, I'd picked up any things that might be
helpful to us. Pat played in the NFL for a couple of years and
started coaching in the NFL in 1979, but he's still willing to
learn.

Then I went up to Parcells's office and we sat and talked
for more than an hour. He told me what bad shape the return
game was in and how much he needed someone who could
straighten it out. He said he could have gotten Henry Ellard,
who'd been a star with the Rams. "But we wanted you,"
Parcells said. I guess the Rams wanted more than a blocking
dummy and a couple of clipboards for Ellard.

He asked me about the Minnesota Vikings, who had just
beaten the Packers, because the Giants would be facing the

Vikings in about six weeks. "I think they'll be tough," Parcells said.

"Oh, you don't have to worry about them," I said.

The next day, I saw my teammates. I think the one who was happiest to see me was Tony Galbreath. He told me he was too old to be returning punts, he didn't ever want to have to do that again.

The night before my first game back with the Giants, I was so hyper I couldn't fall asleep until after midnight. Then, about four o'clock in the morning, I got up to go to the bathroom and I walked into the door and cut my head. Between the excitement and the bleeding, I couldn't get back to sleep. It was a good thing I didn't have a roommate.

It was a good thing, too, that I'd had a lot of rest in Green Bay, because in St. Louis, against the Cardinals, I was busy. I returned seven punts for 82 yards. I gained more than twice as many yards on punt returns in one game as the whole team gained in its first four games.

Some people seemed surprised I did so well, after not returning a punt the whole time I was out there in Green Bay, but it's not something you forget how to do. I practiced every day. And I studied. I studied films of Ivan Arapostathis, the Cardinals' punter, during the week of the game. He'd been kicking short all season, and he didn't have great hang time, either. So I dropped back 40 yards instead of the usual 45, and when he averaged less than 40 yards a punt against us, I was in perfect position to get off good returns.

I had only one pass thrown to me, and I tried to make a diving catch. I had the ball in my hands, but as I hit the ground, the ball squirted loose. I shouldn't have dropped it. Diving catches are my specialty.

It was basically a defensive game, and my punt returns, and Sean Landeta's punts, played a big part in the victory. Sean averaged almost 48 yards a punt, which is awesome. Raul Allegre went two for two on field goals, from 44 yards and 31, so our kicking game seemed solid.

Carl Banks was all over the field. He had ten tackles, including two sacks. He's a linebacker from Michigan State, a first-round choice in 1984, and he's already almost as good as Lawrence. Carl is big and powerful and ferocious on the field, but off the field, he's always cheerful, always nice to everyone. He's very gentle. We have a lot of strong, gentle people on our team.

Not Lawrence. L.T. is never gentle.

After the game, in the locker room, when Parcells got up in front of the team before the press came in, he called out, "Hey, McConkey, where are you? Get up here." He made me stand up and singled me out and made me feel special. A lot of coaches would be reluctant to do that, to give credit to someone they had cut earlier in the year. A lot of teams wouldn't have brought back a guy they cut. They would've been afraid it would be like admitting a mistake. Bringing me back showed how serious the Giants were about winning in 1986. They weren't worried about appearances. They were worried about results.

I was glad I was able to contribute. I was glad I was back.

SIMMS A few days after the St. Louis game, the front office made another move that showed how serious the Giants were about wanting to win in 1986. They gave up two future draft choices to get Ottis Anderson from the Cardinals. O.J. was one of the six players drafted ahead of me in 1979, and he became one of the best runners in the NFL. He was no longer quite as fast as he once was, but he was still talented, still dangerous. He gave us the perfect backup to Joe Morris.

CONKS Before the next game, against Philadelphia, my first home game in 1986, I was the first guy to go on the field. I sprinted down the sidelines. As I reached the end zone, the crowd cheered, welcoming me back, and I waved, and the cheers grew louder, and from then on, that was my pre-game ritual—racing in front of the stands, stirring up the fans, firing a fist or two in the air. It got the adrenaline going, the fans' and mine.

I needed it.

I'm an adrenaline addict.

SIMMS Our fifth victory in a row was our first really easy one, 35–3, over the Eagles. I passed for two touchdowns—to rookie Solomon Miller and to Lee Rouson, the first touchdowns of their careers—and I ran for one, and on a fake field goal attempt, Jeff Rutledge threw a touchdown pass to Harry Carson, Harry's third touchdown in eleven seasons. Lawrence Taylor sacked their quarterbacks four times, and Ottis Anderson, in his debut as a Giant, gained 32 yards in seven carries.

But Ottis also pulled a hamstring, Bavaro sprained a toe, Stacy Robinson sprained an ankle and Bobby Johnson, who was limping, didn't catch a pass.

We thought about making Harry Carson a wideout.

CONKS I cracked a rib against the Eagles. It wasn't broken, it wasn't going to stick through a lung or anything, so there wasn't much I could do about it. I just played with it, played through the pain. It was no big deal. Everybody in pro football plays in pain, and I wasn't going to take any chance on sitting down and having somebody take my place. Besides, I caught two passes from Simms, and that's the best painkiller in the world.

People say I've got a high threshold of pain, but in my mind, I don't. I think I'm a baby. I complain all the time. When I was a kid, if I got a cold, I'd go running to my mother, and I still do.

Simms is the one with the high threshold of pain. I've seen him lying on the training table black and blue from head to toe. His left shoulder, his blind side, is just a bruised mess. His hands look like elephant skin, from banging against so many helmets. I don't know how he takes it.

Simms and I live on Advil sometimes. As far as we're concerned, that's the drug of choice. That's our only drug.

SIMMS Seattle ended our winning streak at five games, which was our longest since I'd been a Giant. The Seahawks beat us, 17–12. I got sacked six times, and four of the sacks were my own fault. Ron Erhardt said that only two of them were my fault, but he was being kind. I thought I could just step into the pocket like I normally do, but Seattle was waiting for me. Jacob Green, a defensive end, sacked me four times. Karl Nelson was trying to handle Green pretty much by himself. Mark Bavaro couldn't play. You don't think I missed him? I threw four interceptions. I missed Lionel and Stacy, too.

CONKS I made a running block on a linebacker on a screen pass to Lee Rouson early in the game, and when I hit the guy, who was about twice my size, I felt my left shoulder pop out. I didn't know what it was till I got to the sidelines. I'd never separated a shoulder before.

The doctor asked me if I wanted to stay in the game. "It's stable," he said. "You can't really do any more damage to it. But it's certainly not 100 percent. It's got to hurt. It's up to you if you want to stay in."

The Giants don't shoot people up when they're in pain. I mean, it's unheard of. The coaches are against it, the trainers are against it, the management is against it.

I was staying in. Even if the doctor had told me to come out, I would've argued with him. With Stacy and Lionel out, I was playing a lot. No way was I coming out.

I felt like I was dragging my shoulder the rest of the game, that I was trying to protect it, but it didn't stop me from catching three passes from Simms. One of them was a real big play.

SIMMS I thought we were going to pull out the game. We were driving in the closing minutes, and on third and long, Conks was going over the middle. I told him, "McConk, if it's close, I'm going to go in there."

I saw the play developing, and I knew that if I threw to McConkey, he was going to get killed. I also knew that, no matter how hard they hit him, he'd catch the ball. I threw to McConkey.

CONKS He drilled it in. I had three guys around me, just like in the playoff game in January against Chicago. That time, Gary Fencik hit me with all he had, and I was up in the air, still holding on to the ball, and then Mike Singletary hit me with all he had, and my bones came loose, but the ball didn't.

This time, again, I took the hits and I held on to the ball. It must have hurt, but the adrenaline was flowing, and the adrenaline killed the pain. I felt terrific.

SIMMS He came back to the huddle, and I said, "You okay, Conks?" I felt a little bad about throwing to him—not as bad as I would've felt if he had dropped the ball—and he said, "Yeah, I'm okay." He's a tough little bastard. My father calls him a game little rascal.

I completed another pass, got us down inside the Seattle twenty, and then I had Solomon Miller open for a touchdown, but I threw the ball so damned hard there was no way he could hold on. My adrenaline was flowing, too. I was so pumped up, I threw the ball too hard, and the drive died, and so did our winning streak.

CONKS While we were losing to Seattle, the Minnesota Vikings were beating Chicago, the Bears' second loss in two years. They had won twelve in a row, including the Super Bowl. "You still think we don't have to worry about the Vikings?" Parcells asked me.

SIMMS McConkey came by the house the other day and saw a picture of Christopher's kindergarten class and said he wanted to meet the teacher. Diana said he couldn't—not until Christopher's in first grade, anyway.

■ The Giants won their next three games in a row, starting a winning streak that would stretch through Super Bowl XXI, but for Phil Simms, who didn't know that the best of times were coming, it was the worst of times. His corps of receivers was depleted. His only reasonably healthy wideouts were rookies, Solomon Miller and Vince Warren. Bobby Johnson couldn't cut without pain. Phil McConkey couldn't cough without pain.

Out of choice and necessity, the Giants' offense turned conservative. The defense turned ferocious.

Joe Morris carried the ball eighty-seven times in the three games and gained 473 yards, more than 100 in each game. He also scored two touchdowns in each game.

Lawrence Taylor made twenty-seven tackles in the three games, nineteen of them unassisted, seven of them quarterback sacks. The defense permitted only two touchdowns in each game.

Simms, by his own standards, did nothing.

Against Washington, he completed twenty passes, but twelve were to running backs, five to the tight end, only three to wide receivers.

Against Dallas, he completed only six of eighteen passes for only 67 yards, his first sub-100-yard game since he regained the starting job in 1984. "We won the game," Simms said afterward, "and I felt like we lost." The Giant fans buried him in boos.

"Joe Morris is their offense," said Tom Landry, the Dallas coach.

Against Philadelphia, Simms completed only eight of eighteen passes for 130 yards. Never since his rookie season had Simms, as a starter, thrown fewer than twenty passes two games in a row.

He threw only one touchdown pass in the three games. He threw three interceptions. He was sacked nine times.

Simms's quarterback rating, based on a complicated formula that includes almost every passing statistic, slipped to 69.0, its lowest level in three years. He ranked ninth among the fourteen starting quarterbacks in the National Conference. He wasn't even in the top twenty in the NFL.

The other quarterback who played his home games in Giants Stadium, Ken O'Brien of the New York Jets, owned the best rating in professional football, 111.1. The Jets owned the best record in pro football, nine and one.

The press and the public made the inevitable comparisons, and even though his teammates defended his skills and his courage, Simms suffered.

SIMMS I was always confident, sometimes too confident. I always thought I could throw the ball in anywhere. But during that dry spell in the middle of the 1986 season, I started doubting myself. Even in the Washington game, when I threw pretty well, I wasn't able to relax, I wasn't able to enjoy it.

In the Dallas game, almost every play I wondered if I was going to do something wrong. It got to the point where I was happy if I threw a pass and it wasn't intercepted. It didn't make any difference whether it was complete or not. I was passing so infrequently, I had no groove, no rhythm.

In the Philadelphia game, I was even more tentative. I just wasn't me. I thought I could sense some of my teammates and coaches losing confidence in me, or at least worrying about me, and that hurt. I knew I could sense some of the fans losing confidence in me.

The booing in the Dallas game, coming on top of my own insecurity, really got to me, maybe for the first time in my career. Well, not the first time. But the *worst* time. In my early years, when the fans booed, it hurt my family more than me. I knew that some of the time I sort of deserved it, and some of the time they weren't really booing me, they were booing the team. We were a bad team. It wouldn't have been easy to cheer us.

But by 1986, we were a good team. We were very good, and the fans were very impatient. I wanted to tell them: Look, we've got people hurt. We can't do some of the things we'd like to do. We're winning with Joe Morris and with defense, and we've got to stick to that because we want to keep winning.

All of that should have been obvious. But it wasn't.

One of my strengths as a quarterback is that I love to play football. I enjoy the competition, the challenge, the camaraderie. I'd rather be taking a snap from center than doing almost anything else in the world. But for a while, in the middle of our Super Bowl season, I didn't love football at all. I almost dreaded going to the stadium.

CONKS The guy in the club in Lodi, New Jersey, was bad-mouthing Simms. "Your buddy Simms," he called him. "He can't even pass for a hundred yards in a game." The guy was louder than the music. He looked like he might have played football in high school, a lineman probably, a big guy, black hair pushed back, tight pants, an open shirt exposing several strands of gold chains.

"We're running the ball," I said, "and it's working."

The guy brushed against me. "He can't win the big ones," the guy said.

I was so sick of hearing the same stupid lines. "He beat Washington and Dallas," I said.

The guy wouldn't let up. "He's a loser," he said. "He's always been a loser." He was instigating, looking for trouble. He half-pushed me, and I turned toward him, and as I turned, I swung my elbow and my forearm around. I guess I pivoted too quickly. I caught him in the chest, and he fell back, threw his arms up in the air and landed flat on the floor.

The bouncer in the club stepped in, and it was all over. People looked at me and nodded as if to tell me the guy was really asking for it.

Guess who showed up in New York a few days after the Washington game? Lesley. The girl I'd lived with in Virginia in 1982. She'd been modeling in Japan, and when she came to New York, she saw me in a commercial and got in touch with me. I was glad to hear from her. I went out with her a couple of times.

I really didn't have time for much of a social schedule. Most days, I stayed at Giants Stadium from early in the morning till early in the evening, and then I had an hour's ride back to Ronnie Barnes's house in East Brunswick, and by the time I got there, I was beat. The weekends were shot because of the games, so the only night I really had free was Monday nights.

There just wasn't much to do in New Jersey on Monday nights.

SIMMS Landeta didn't have any trouble finding things to do on Monday night. Or Tuesday night or Wednesday night or Thursday night or Friday night. Landeta was leading the league in punting and a few other things.

CONKS Landeta, Bavaro and I were supposed to be the Italian Stallions of the Giants, three swinging bachelors. Bavaro spend his nights in his hotel room near the stadium. He called his girlfriend in Connecticut just about every night. I spent my nights discussing kinesiology with Ronnie Barnes. Lan-

157

deta had to carry the load for all three of us. He tried. God knows, he tried.

SIMMS On my birthday, the day after we beat Dallas, guys kept coming up to me and saying, "How does it feel to be thirty?" And I kept saying, "I don't know. I'm not thirty anymore. I'm thirty-one."

"But according to the records . . ."

According to the New York Giants, I was born on November 3, 1956. That's the way they've listed me since I was a rookie. I don't know why. I was actually born on November 3, 1955.

I don't mind losing the year. That just means one less year till I can give up this game.

There are only three men on the team who are older than me: George Martin, Harry Carson and Tony Galbreath. I'm three weeks older than Benson. That means I'm the oldest white man on a very young team.

Parcells knew what I was going through, knew I was wondering about myself. He called me into his office a few days after the Philadelphia game. "I don't know what you're thinking," he said, "but here's what I think: I think you're a great quarterback, and you got that way by being daring and fearless. Just go back to being that way. Be the sort of quarterback that has the other guys worrying on Saturday night."

He pumped me up when I needed it.

I got another pep talk the night before we played the Vikings, this one from Terry Bradshaw. He was broadcasting the game and staying in the same hotel we were. He asked me to stop by his room to say hello, and we talked about my slump, and the fans booing, and Terry said, "People don't understand what it takes to be a quarterback, what you got to go through."

158

He told me about his slumps and how he played his way through them, and how he ignored the critics, and then he said, "I'll tell you something about tomorrow's game. You guys are gonna win it throwing the ball, and you're gonna make the big plays. No doubt about it. You're gonna be the hero. I know."

Don't forget—Terry Bradshaw was my hero. Terry and Roger Staubach, they were the only sports heroes I ever had. I saw Terry win four Super Bowls, three on television and one in person, and what he said pumped me up just as much as what Parcells said.

CONKS Raul Allegre was sitting by himself in the coffee shop of our hotel in Minneapolis. Gary Reasons, the captain of the special teams, spotted him and asked him why he was eating alone. Raul said he didn't feel like part of the team. He didn't think he had done anything to contribute to the team. In the previous five games he had kicked six field goals, but three of them were just glorified extra points, and he had missed five, one from inside the 30-yard line. "C'mon, eat with us," Gary said, and over dinner he told Raul that he would kick a field goal to win the game against Minnesota.

SIMMS "The race is on," Parcells told us before the Viking game, the first of four straight games, three of them on the road, against teams that had playoff hopes and Super Bowl dreams.

I was glad that Stacy Robinson was finally back, his ankle healed after missing four games. Still, we intended to establish our running game. But the Vikings were set up to stop Joe Morris, and they did a pretty good job of it.

CONKS At halftime we led 9–6, and all the scoring was on field goals. Allegre hit three in a row, from 41 yards, 37 and 24, and then, on the last play of the half, missed from 60 yards out.

On one of Allegre's kickoffs, a short squib kick, Solomon Miller, the rookie wideout, impressed the hell out of me. He went downfield like a torpedo, barreled full speed into a Minnesota lineman who was reaching to pick up the ball and knocked the guy, who must've outweighed him by a hundred pounds, into the middle of next week.

SIMMS Fran Tarkenton was presented with his Hall of Fame ring at halftime. Tarkenton played eighteen seasons in the NFL, five with the Giants, thirteen with the Vikings. He threw more passes, completed more passes and gained more yards than any other quarterback in the history of the game. By huge margins.

But if you don't count the 1982 and 1983 seasons, when I was hurt, I had thrown more passes, completed more passes and gained more yards in my first five Giant seasons than Tarkenton had in his five.

Still, I don't think anybody's ever going to give me a Hall of Fame ring.

(Unless Fran wants to make a trade for a Super Bowl ring.)

CONKS Minnesota took a 13–9 lead in the third quarter, but in the fourth, after Allegre kicked his fourth field goal, Simms hit Bobby Johnson for a touchdown that put us in front, 19–13.

SIMMS For the third game in a row, the opposing quarterback went down with an injury. Dallas had lost Danny White when Carl Banks sacked him and broke his wrist. Philadelphia had lost Ron Jaworski when he smacked his throwing hand on a helmet and tore a tendon in his finger. Minnesota lost Tommy Kramer when he hit Lawrence Taylor's helmet and jammed his right thumb. Wade Wilson came off the bench and threw a 33-yard touchdown pass to Anthony Carter. They went ahead, 20–19, with less than seven mintues to play.

CONKS We got the ball at our own 41-yard line, with a little more than two minutes left in the game. Stacy ran a "go" down the right sideline, and Simms led him perfectly. If Stacy had made the catch, he would've scored or come damn close. But the ball bounced off his arms. He was still a little rusty. We all know that feeling.

We picked up a first down, moved into Minnesota territory, but on third and eight at the Viking 43, Doug Martin, George's kid brother, broke through and sacked Simms on our 48.

It was fourth-and-seventeen with a minute and twelve seconds to play.

If we didn't make the first down, the Vikings would run out the clock, and our winning streak would be dead.

Parcells called a timeout.

SIMMS I went to the sidelines. Parcells and Hodgson were on the phone, talking to Erhardt, who was up in the press box. Ron suggested the play. Hodgson offered a modification. "Why not put McConkey in motion?" Pat said. "That would make them change their formation and maybe make the safeties screw up."

"Good idea," Parcells said. "Let's do it."

I went back to the huddle. "Half right, W motion, seventy-four," I said. "We need seventeen yards. Just be sure it's seventeen."

The play called for Stacy Robinson, split to the left, to run straight downfield, then cut sharply to the inside; for Mc-Conkey, lined up in the slot to the left, to go in motion to the right, run straight downfield, then cut diagonally to the inside;

for Tony Galbreath, in the backfield, to slip past the line of scrimmage, into the middle; for Mark Bavaro, on the right, one step behind the line of scrimmage, to run straight downfield, but not deep; and for Bobby Johnson, split to the right, to run straight downfield, then turn to the sideline.

I thought Bobby Johnson was my best bet, if I could get the ball to him.

The Vikings, concerned only with preventing the first down, were using six defensive backs. Two guarded the first-down area in front of Bobby.

I crouched behind the center—the crowd was too loud for us to use the shotgun—took the snap, dropped back and waited for the wide receivers to get downfield. Bavaro saw that Minnesota's left tackle was trying to loop around the end to get to me, so Mark stayed in place and blocked. Mike Stensrud, playing right tackle for Minnesota, charged up the middle. The year before, when Stensrud was playing for Houston, I'd cut my little finger on his face mask.

When I looked at Stacy, he wasn't open. I didn't have time to look at him again. I saw Bobby go past the first-down marker. I saw him stop and turn to me. I knew I had to get the ball over the defensive back in front of him. Stensrud was about to hit me. I threw, and as I did, as I went down, I knew that I'd thrown the ball just the way I wanted to.

I saw the films later. Bobby had to wait for the ball. He couldn't come back to it because if he did, he might lose the first-down yardage. The ball just floated over the fingers of Issiac Holt, the defensive back in front of Johnson. John Harris, the safety, playing on the inside of Johnson, drawn to the inside by McConkey's move, couldn't quite recover in time.

Bobby planted himself, made certain his feet were in bounds, caught the ball, then stepped out, stopping the clock.

The play gained 22 yards.

The odds against us were enormous. If I threw that pass a hundred times, I'd get it to Bobby maybe five times or six. This was one of those times.

We had the first down at the Minnesota 30.

We had plenty of time left to win the game.

CONKS When Bobby caught The Pass, I knew we'd win the game. During the timeout before The Pass, the guys on the Minnesota bench had been laughing and joking, confident of victory. They weren't laughing anymore.

We moved the ball down to the 15-yard line, in the middle of the field, and with twelve seconds to play, Raul Allegre kicked a 33-yard field goal, his fifth in six attempts, to win the game, 22–20. Gary Reasons grabbed Allegre and hugged him.

I went crazy, jumping up and down and pumping my fist as I ran off the field. So did most of my teammates. It was the only time all season, till the Super Bowl, that we really celebrated a victory. "It looks like a Giants-Mets year," Jim Burt shouted, two weeks after the Mets won the World Series, and nobody argued with him.

Reasons asked Parcells to give Allegre a game ball, which is something we hardly ever do, and Parcells did it. Allegre was on top of the world. He wasn't going to eat alone anymore.

SIMMS Parcells kissed me as I came into the locker room. "You can play on my team anytime," he said.

Everybody kept talking about the fourth-and-seventeen pass. Benson said he had his back to the play, but when he heard the crowd making no noise, he knew we'd made the first down. Bart Oates said he turned around after his block just in time to see the catch. Karl Nelson said, "What play?"

Karl was hit in the head on the previous play and he didn't remember the call or the pass or the completion. "Fourth down?" he said. "Really?"

Really.

CONKS Simms completed twenty-five of thirty-eight passes for 310 yards. He completed eight passes to his wideouts for 143 yards, including two to me for 41 yards. He had two passes dropped that might've gone for touchdowns. Parcells couldn't resist needling the reporters who'd been writing things all week like, "What is the problem with Phil Simms, anyway?"

"Anybody who doesn't think Phil Simms is a great quarterback should be covering another sport," Parcells said.

SIMMS When I got home, close to ten o'clock that night, I told Diana, "I want to see the tape," and I went into the family room and sat down and, after a month of not looking at the tapes of any of our games, I watched from beginning to end. And it wasn't just because I wanted to hear how Terry Bradshaw did.

It was a helluva play, fourth-and-seventeen.

CONKS Simms and I celebrated the Minnesota victory by lifting weights the next day. Everybody is expected to lift twice a week during the season, but Phil and I like to go in four days —Monday, Tuesday, Thursday and Friday. On Friday, I generally just watch because I want my legs to be fresh on Sunday. I have to worry about residual fatigue. Simms doesn't have to worry about the spring in his legs.

Johnny Parker keeps us on four-week cycles, and what we do each day is based on percentages of our target weights, the goals we set for ourselves with Johnny's guidance. We do a power-lifting program, power cleans, power snatches, squats, bench presses, lots of different things, but the principle is always the same: we start the cycle with more repetitions and less weight, progress to fewer repetitions and more weight and then, in the fourth week, cut back, taper off, give our bodies a chance to recover and to build up. Johnny doesn't want us to overtrain. He feels, like the Russians, that most American athletes do. I know I did, until I met him, and he showed me that his methods work.

Simms and I got to the stadium around eleven the morning

after the Viking game, our usual time, and after we'd finished lifting, we were sitting in the steam, relaxing, when Erhardt and Hodgson said they wanted to see us. They wanted to show us something they'd spotted while they were studying the films of the Broncos.

Basically, this is what they found. When I lined up in the slot, on third down with more than five yards to go, Denver would have a defensive back playing over me and a linebacker playing inside him. Normally, if the guy over me blitzed, the guy inside him blitzed, too. That was the way most teams worked it, and if I saw that happening, I had to sight-adjust. That is, I had to cut my route short, so that Simms could get rid of the ball quickly, before one of those guys blitzing hit him in the mouth.

But Denver sometimes would try a trick. Sometimes the guy over me blitzed, and the guy inside him didn't. That guy fell back into short pass coverage. They wanted me to run a short route and get short yardage. The coaches told me that if only the guy over me blitzed, our blocking back would pick him up, Simms would have more time and I should run my full route.

Erhardt and Hodgson ran the films back and forth, showing us the options. They said it was up to me to know when to cut my route short and when to run the full route.

SIMMS O. J. Anderson fit in just perfect on our team. He didn't play a whole lot, but he didn't bitch, he didn't cause any trouble, he didn't act like the superstar he is. "Hey, I'm a relief pitcher," he said, and it was good to know we had him just in case.

CONKS Denver came into Giants Stadium with a nine-and-two record, the same as ours, and late in the first half, they were leading, 6–3, and driving toward a touchdown. They had a first down on our 13-yard line. John Elway, their quarterback, dropped back, then lofted a little swing pass toward one of his running backs.

George Martin leaped up and, like the basketball player he had been at the University of Oregon, tipped the ball, grabbed it and started down the sideline toward the goal line, 78 yards away. Near midfield, he brushed aside Elway's attempt to tackle him. George was thirty-three, an eleventh-round draft choice in his twelfth NFL season.

Deep into Denver territory, running out of steam, he thought of lateraling the ball to Lawrence Taylor, who was six years younger. But then George remembered that the defense had put up a $1,000 pot for the first defensive player to score a touchdown in 1986. Harry Carson had scored on an offensive play, which didn't count. Nobody had scored yet on a fumble return or an interception. George held on to the ball.

L.T. tackled him—in the end zone. George had the seventh touchdown of his career, his sixth on defense, an NFL record for defensive linemen, and we had a 10–6 lead at the half.

SIMMS Denver's defense was tough. Joe Morris had to fight for every yard he got, I couldn't find a wide receiver open and even Bavaro was having trouble getting free. He caught only one pass all day, his least productive game of the season.

Of course, our defense was tough, too, and even though Elway was throwing much more than me, and completing much more—he is a hell of a quarterback—neither offense had scored a touchdown going into the fourth quarter.

In the third quarter, Raul Allegre kicked a 45-yard field goal for us, and Rich Karlis a 42-yarder for them, so we had a 13–9 lead.

CONKS In the fourth quarter, on a third down and six to go, I lined up in the slot to the left. The Broncos had a defensive back playing over me, and a linebacker playing inside him.

On the snap, they both blitzed and I sight-adjusted. I cut my pattern short and Simms hit me for 8 yards and a first down. We moved into field goal range, and Allegre kicked a 46-yarder that gave us a 16–9 lead.

SIMMS Elway marched the Broncos more than 70 yards to tie the score. He completed five passes on the first seven plays of the drive. He had his biggest day of the season—the most passes, the most completions, the most yards passing and the most yards running—and when he was finished, there was less than two minutes to play.

CONKS I ran the kickoff back to the 29-yard line, but then we got pushed back to the 18, third and twenty-one, and Simms did it again. He found Bobby Johnson down the middle for 24 yards, just a routine miracle after the big miracle against Minnesota. Bobby got hit so hard, he didn't know where he was. I helped him up.

But again we lost a few yards, back to our 39, second and thirteen. I lined up in the slot to the left. The Broncos had a defensive back playing over me, and a linebacker playing inside him. On the snap, the defensive back blitzed. But the linebacker didn't. I saw him fall back, and I ran my full route, straight down the field, straight down the seam of the Denver zone.

Tony Galbreath put a beautiful block on the blitzing defensive back, and Simms, with plenty of time, fired a perfect pass. I was wide open. I took the ball down to the 15-yard line, a 46-yard gain.

We ran the ball to the middle of the field, let the clock run down and then Allegre kicked his fourth straight field goal, this one from 34 yards, and we had a 19–16 victory.

The fans went crazy. We took this one a little more in stride. We had won ten games, eight of them by seven points or less.

SIMMS As we were running off the field, John Elway came up to me and said, "I hope we face you again." I kind of shook my head. "I'm not sure I want to face your defense again," I said.

CONKS I came out of the stadium after the Denver game and found a young woman waiting by my car. She told me she was a journalism major at Rutgers and she had requested credentials to cover the game, but the Giants had turned her down. She said she wanted to interview me for her college paper. I felt sorry for her. She was very cute. I told her I would meet her on Monday, after I worked out, and she could interview me over lunch.

The next day we went to a Chinese restaurant, and she started asking me questions. I noticed that she didn't have a tape recorder or a pen or a pencil or a pad. "Are you giving me a line about that reporter bit?" I said. "Or do you just have a tremendous memory? I've been around some reporters, you know, and they usually record."

She confessed that she didn't go to Rutgers and she wasn't a journalism major, she just wanted to meet me. "I couldn't think of any other way," she said.

She was so cute, I just laughed.

I didn't go out with her, though. I didn't have the time.

SIMMS I went home after the Denver game and just ate a little corned-beef hash. Normally, I love to eat, but I never have a great appetite after a game. I have to force it down.

Diana and I used to go out on Sunday nights, with some of the other guys and their wives, but I stopped doing that in 1984. It wasn't a good idea. One guy might be in a good mood, another guy in a bad mood, and sometimes it got real uncomfortable.

The longer I've played, the more I've wanted to lead a separate life away from the field. I spend so much time with my teammates anyway, eight or nine hours almost every day. Then, if we go out, we end up talking football, and it's not fair to the wives. It's bad enough they've got to answer football questions in the supermarket and the beauty parlor.

Now I just stay at home with Diana every Sunday night. I'm sore, usually, and I sit in front of the TV and watch the sports shows. I can't go to sleep till I replay the game in my head. The better I played, the less sleep I get.

CONKS The Los Angeles Rams dropped Rob Carpenter in mid-season. He'd been covering kicks for the first time in his career, not playing at all on offense. Ironically, if he'd stayed with us, he probably would've played a lot after George Adams got hurt.

SIMMS I figured the 49ers had everything going for them. We were playing in San Francisco, a Monday-night game, and they needed to win, and they had Joe Montana back. He'd started playing only fifty-five days after back surgery that was supposed to end his career, and in his first three games he'd completed sixty-seven of 111 passes for 943 yards. Those numbers were the best advertisement for back surgery I'd ever seen.

In the first half, Montana led the 49ers on three long scoring drives, ending one with a touchdown pass to Jerry Rice. They had a 17–0 lead at the half, and a lot of people back East were ready to turn their TVs off.

CONKS Mark Bavaro turned the game around. Bavaro and Simms. Phil did it with a series of super passes. Mark did it with one play. Early in the third quarter, Simms threw a short pass, and Mark caught the ball at the San Francisco 40-yard line and carried it all the way to the 18. Six different 49ers hit him hard along the way. He carried Ronnie Lott, the safety, on his back for 14 yards. He carried Keena Turner, the linebacker, for eight. It took four men, finally, to drag him down. It was awesome. I'd never seen anything like it.

Right after that, Simms hit Joe Morris for 17 yards and a touchdown, and we were on our way back.

SIMMS We got the ball right back, moved to midfield, then bogged down. On fourth-and-two, I turned to tell Parcells I wanted to go for it, and he was already sending the play in. Flow thirty-eight. A running play for Joe Morris.

Joe was having his toughest game of the season. He had carried the ball nine times up till then and had gained zero yards. On fourth-and-two, he gained 17.

The next play, I hit Stacy Robinson for 34 yards and a touchdown, and we were only three points down. I trotted off the field feeling pretty good. "You still got another one to get," said Parcells.

It didn't take long. The 49ers got three plays and a punt, and then I hit Carthon for 7, McConkey for 14 and Robinson for 49, down to the San Francisco one-yard line. I handed the ball to Ottis Anderson and he drove into the end zone for the first touchdown of his New York Giant career.

We had scored three touchdowns in nine minutes, the best nine minutes I ever played. We were ahead, 21–17.

CONKS We won, 21–17, our ninth victory by seven points or less.

I played most of the game with a taped-up broken thumb, and I still managed to have my best game of the season. I caught two passes for 46 yards, returned three kickoffs for 65 yards and returned three punts for 34 yards, 145 total yards. Good numbers for me.

Simms's numbers were sensational. He completed twenty-seven of thirty-eight passes for 388 yards and two touchdowns, his fourth 300-yard game of the season.

Bavaro's were sensational, too, seven receptions for 98

yards. Mark's father, who'd also played for Notre Dame, had been drafted by the 49ers but didn't make the team, so maybe Mark decided to show San Francisco what the Bavaros were like.

Mark and I talked on the plane coming home. We talked mostly about religion. Mark studied religion at Notre Dame, and he tries to answer my questions. Mark's very intelligent. He's also very gentle, although I don't suppose the 49ers would agree with that.

SIMMS People asked me after the San Francisco game what adjustments we made at halftime. I tied my shoelaces, that was the only adjustment I made. Halftime speech? I haven't heard a halftime speech since college. We don't get much of a pre-game speech, either. Parcells just tells us to go out there and kick ass.

CONKS "What do you think?" Parcells asked me in the empty locker room. "You think guys around here are getting big heads?" He looked worried. "We're getting too many stars here," he said, "and you're one of them."

"You don't have to worry about me," I said. "I know I'm always one play away from being out on the street."

"Not if you keep making the plays you're making," he said.

For Parcells, that was a huge compliment.

SIMMS Brad Benson turned to me in the steam room a couple of days after the San Francisco game and whispered, "Well, this is gonna be my last season." He said his back hurt, his knees hurt and his nose hurt. "I'm just gonna pack it in," he said, very confidentially.

Benson also told me he was going to pack it in in 1985, 1984 and 1983. He always acted as if I was the only one he was telling it to. He told it to everyone.

A few days after his annual pack-it-in speech, Benson started his seventy-fifth straight game, at tackle or guard, against the Washington Redskins.

You'll have to kill him before he quits.

CONKS I was already on the field, catching punts, when Simms came out to loosen up. The crowd at R.F.K. Stadium in Washington greeted him with boos. "Great," Simms said. "They're making me feel just like I'm at home."

SIMMS The Washington game was probably going to decide the division championship. We knew the Redskins were good. We knew that, like us, they had won eleven of thirteen games. Yet we were confident. After the way we'd come from behind to win the Minnesota, Denver and San Francisco games, we *had* to be confident.

Still, in the last two minutes of the first half, the score was tied, 7–7, and we faced one of those situations we were getting accustomed to—third and seven at our own 40-yard line. "To heck with a first down," Parcells said. "Let's go deep. I want it all."

He was just like the rest of us. He was beginning to believe that we could do anything.

I called eighty-two go, sent all the receivers deep and passed to Bobby Johnson for 34 yards. Two plays later, I hit Bobby for a touchdown and a 14–7 lead at the half.

CONKS Lawrence Taylor sacked their quarterback, Jay Schroeder, three times. "When he hits you," Schroeder said, "you have to take inventory." He was counting his arms and legs all day. Schroeder was intercepted six times, and on one of the interceptions, late in the third quarter, Harry Carson returned the ball deep into Redskin territory.

Three plays later, from the 16-yard line, I raced into the left-hand corner of the end zone and Simms drilled the ball between two Redskin defenders. I was playing with a little piece of plastic taped to the back of my broken thumb to give it some stability. I couldn't quite form the V I like to form with my thumbs and forefingers when I make a catch.

Darrell Green, closing fast, reached out and barely touched the ball, just slightly changing its course.

I juggled the ball.

I bobbled it.

I caught it.

When you score only one touchdown each season, you can't make it just a routine touchdown. You have to make it look good. I made my 1986 touchdown look spectacular. It ended up on all the highlight films.

That gave us a 24–7 lead, and we coasted to a 24–14 victory.

SIMMS All week long, Dexter Manley, the Redskins' defensive end who had been leading the league in sacks, had been talking about what he was going to do to me, but in the game, Dexter didn't do anything. He had only two tackles and no sacks. Benson played opposite him. Benson played a great game. "I feel like I'm sucking eggs," Manley said afterward.

CONKS Terry Kinard, the Giants' number-one draft choice in 1983, a starting safety for four years, went down with an injury in the Washington game. He was out for the rest of the season. We needed a defensive back. Parcells called me at Ronnie's house and asked me about Tom Flynn, who had been my teammate in Green Bay.

Flynn, from the University of Pittsburgh, made the All-Rookie team in 1984, was a starter in 1985 and was dropped by the Packers in 1986. Forrest Gregg didn't think he was intimidating enough. "Can he tackle?" Parcells asked.

"Yeah, he can tackle," I said. "He can play."

"You better be right," Parcells said, "or it's your ass."

I'd had dinner with Flynn and his wife in Green Bay. I liked him. I thought he could help us.

Parcells signed him to play on the special teams and to back up Herb Welch, who was moving into Kinard's place.

SIMMS Brad Benson was named the National Football Conference offensive player of the week for his performance against Dexter Manley. It was the first time in the three-year history of the award that they gave it to a lineman. To celebrate, the rest of our offensive line put bandages on their noses.

And each of them announced that he was going to pack it in after this season.

CONKS Johnny Parker came up to me in the weight room and told me I was a 95 percenter. I thought he was complimenting me on my lifts. "What's a 95 percenter?" I asked him.

"Ninety-five percent of why girls go out with you is that you're a football player," Parker said.

SIMMS The day before we played St. Louis in our next-to-last game of the regular season, Denver beat Washington, which meant that we clinched the division championship, the first title of any kind for the Giants in twenty-three years. But we still knew that we had to win our last two games to make certain that we had the home-field advantage for all our play-off games.

We beat St. Louis easily. I didn't do much. The story was the familiar one, Joe Morris and the defense. Joe ran for 179 yards and three touchdowns, his biggest day of the season, and the defense sacked Neil Lomax nine times, a record for the Giants.

CONKS I'd become a regular on Z-100, every Monday morning, either coming in myself or calling the station to give my report on the game the day before and to chat with Scott Shannon and some of their other people. I'd been listening to the station for three years, since my first training camp—it was my kind of top-forty music—and I probably would've done the reports for nothing. But Fishof had me getting paid.

Scott picked on me all the time. Once he called Warner Wolf, the sportscaster—you know, "Let's go to the videotape"—and he asked Warner, on the air, what his favorite Phil McConkey highlight was, and Warner said he was sorry, but he didn't have any Phil McConkey highlights.

I took phone calls from listeners, too, and the day after the St. Louis game, one guy called and said he was Harry Finkelstein from Brooklyn and he had a question for me. "Is it true," he said, "that you go into Mark Bavaro's locker and look through his discarded mail and pick up all the ones with pictures of girls inside?"

I figured it had to be someone who knew our locker room because Bavaro had just gotten a picture of a knockout girl in a bathing suit and, of course, being engaged and being Bavaro, he wasn't going to keep the picture and he wasn't going to answer the letter, so I took it, just to show it around.

I finally recognized the voice.

It was Burt.

SIMMS Eight of our guys were named for the Pro Bowl, and to nobody's surprise, L.T. was chosen for the sixth straight year, Harry Carson for the eighth time in nine years, Joe Morris and Leonard Marshall for the second year in a row and Sean Landeta and Mark Bavaro for the first time. But the other two were surprises, pleasant surprises. Brad Benson was named for the first time in his ten-year career, and Jim Burt for the first time in his six years. The whole offensive line wore Brad's uniform number, 60, in his honor, and Burt went around telling everybody, "I used to be a dirtbag, and now I'm an All-Pro."

CONKS Simms didn't bitch, but he should've been named to the Pro Bowl. They chose Montana and Schroeder from the

NFC, and Elway and Marino from the AFC, and Simms went head-to-head against three of the four in 1986 and beat them every time. They may have fancier numbers, but Simms wins. They picked him last year and he ended up being MVP.

Simms has one consolation, anyway. He and I were both named to the All-Madden team, the lineup chosen by John Madden, the former Oakland coach who switched to CBS television. Madden chooses his team for its toughness, its character. "McConkey's always got a 'too' in front of his name," Madden said. "He's too small, too slow, too old. He's what pro football is all about. The average fan can identify with him. The average fan can't identify with the superstars."

SIMMS Mark Gastineau of the Jets and I did a TV commercial together, and as soon as I saw him, I told him, "The worst hit I've taken in my life was from you, and I got up from it."

"The worst hit?" Gastineau said. "You mean the best. It was in 1981, and I came up the middle, and it was the greatest hit I've ever had on a quarterback, and I couldn't believe you got up."

"Man, I don't know how I did," I said. "It just killed me."

Gastineau remembered the details just as clearly as I did, and a lot more fondly. I had a blood sac on my back for two weeks after the hit, and my chest was black and blue for a month. Six years later, I still feel it. I really do. I feel a little pop in my chest about five times a day. I must have a little calcium deposit where Gastineau hit me, a souvenir to make certain I never forget him.

CONKS The smile on Tom Flynn's face told the whole story. In the first quarter against the Green Bay Packers, his former team and mine, Flynn blocked a punt and grabbed the ball

176

and ran 36 yards for a touchdown. For the last 10 or 15 yards, his smile was so broad even Forrest Gregg must have seen it.

We took a 24–0 lead, let them get back within seven points, then finished them off, 55–24.

Gregg had tried to stir up the Packers by telling them that I'd bad-mouthed them, that I'd called them losers. It wasn't true, but it helped make for a pretty nasty game.

■ Only twice in their history, only once in fifty years, had the New York Giants scored more than 55 points in a game.

The Giants had a nine-game winning streak.

The Giants had a fourteen-and-two record, matching the Chicago Bears for the best in the NFL.

The Giants had the home-field advantage for all the playoff games leading up to the Super Bowl.

The Giants also had a flock of outstanding individual statistics:

Joe Morris ran for 1,516 yards, breaking his own Giant record for one season.

Mark Bavaro caught sixty-six passes for 1,001 yards, both records for a Giant tight end.

Sean Landeta averaged 44.8 yards a punt, the best in the National Football Conference.

Lawrence Taylor recorded twenty and one-half sacks, the most in pro football.

Phil Simms, who ranked ninth among NFL quarterbacks more than halfway through the season, ranked fourth at the end. His rating climbed from 69.0 to 74.6

(Ironically, Ken O'Brien of the New York Jets, who had ranked first in the American Conference for much of the season, ranked fifth at the end. His rating slipped from 111.1 to 85.8. Not coincidentally, the Jets lost their last five games in a row and barely qualified for the playoffs as a wild-card team.)

Raul Allegre, the Giants' third place-kicker, converted

thirty-three of thirty-three extra-point attempts and twenty-four of thirty-two field goal attempts. He didn't miss a field goal from less than 40 yards in the last seven games of the season.

Phil McConkey, despite missing the first four games, caught sixteen passes for 279 yards, and returned thirty-two punts for 253 yards and twenty-four kickoffs for 471 yards. For the third straight year, he wound up with more than 1,000 all-purpose yards. He just made it, with 1,003. For the second straight year, he did not lose a fumble on a pass reception, a punt return or a kickoff return.

One more significant number: The Giants knew that if they won their two playoff games and the Super Bowl, they would earn $64,000 a man.

And a ring.

They could hardly wait.

SIMMS Nobody had to come to the stadium the Monday after the Green Bay game, but Burt and McConkey showed up early because they knew I was taping a guest VJ spot for MTV, and they were afraid they wouldn't get on. They got on. We were all asked to say why we pour Gatorade on Parcells after each victory, and each of us tried to say something funny, except Burt. " 'Cause I hate him," Burt said.

McConkey kept hanging around the camera. I think he was trying to find out if he could meet Madonna, or any other female singer. After the taping, he came back to my house, ate lamb chops and played with Christopher, who thinks McConkey's the greatest thing in the world. "Who do you want to grow up to be like?" I ask him, and he says, "Phil McConkey," which terrifies Diana.

We watched the Monday-night game, Miami against New England. I kept thinking that before he's finished, Marino will own every passing record in pro football. McConkey kept thinking that he was Stanley Morgan. Morgan made some great catches.

CONKS I got a letter from a girl who enclosed a nude picture of herself and said she'd really like to meet me. She had a dynamite body. But I answered her just the way I answer everybody who writes to me. I sent her an action photo of me in my Giant uniform and I signed it, "Best wishes, Phil Mc-Conkey, # 80."

I'd never do anything more than that because, in the first place, what kind of a girl would send a picture like that, and in the second, how do you know the picture is really of her?

SIMMS With our first playoff game two weeks away, we got a few extra days off at the end of the regular season, and with Christopher home from school for Christmas vacation, we got to spend a little time together. We played catch, of course, and watched some movies on the VCR. We saw *Dumbo* and *Pinocchio* and *Mary Poppins,* and our favorite was *Old Yeller.* Christopher and I must've watched *Old Yeller* three or four times. I never saw any of those movies when I was a kid.

I'd be lying if I didn't say I want Christopher to grow up to be an athlete. Of course I'd like that. But I just want him to grow up to be a good kid, really.

In some ways, he's got it tougher than I did when I was a kid. It's going to be harder for him to be an athlete. I had my four brothers, and our whole world was sports. That was the way we entertained ourselves.

But Christopher's got a million other things. There's not a day goes by that I don't say to Diana, "God, he's got too much," or, "No, don't get him that, he doesn't need that."

It's like a tightwire act. I want him to have some of the things I didn't have, but I don't want him to have too much. I hate it when he acts like a little rich kid, like a spoiled brat.

Sometimes one of the kids down the street'll get something, and Christopher'll say he wants it, too, and I'll say, "No, you can't get everything that the other kids get." It's not easy for me. I almost give in sometimes, but if I don't, a few days later he's forgotten what he asked for.

179

Presents just don't mean as much to him as they did to me. When I was ten years old, I got a red bike for Christmas. My brothers Don and Tommy each got a bike, too. I was just stunned because we didn't have many big Christmases.

I think I still believed in Santa Claus then.

Or maybe I'd just gotten over him.

I knew Diana wanted a diamond watch more than anything for Christmas, but every time she dropped a hint about it, I told her, "No way, no more jewelry, no more furs, none of that stuff." And I meant it, I really did, I'm embarrassed by owning that kind of stuff. Then, the day before Christmas, I went to a jeweler I knew and I bought her a diamond watch.

Christopher and I took the watch over to the pharmacy, and I asked the man there to wrap it for me. When we got home, Diana wanted to know where we'd been, and I told her I took Christopher to the pharmacy to buy her a Christmas present, they've got real pretty fake jewelry there.

After our Christmas Eve dinner, we were going over to a neighbor's house for dessert, and I said, "C'mon, before we go, let's each open up one present." I handed her the watch, and she recognized the wrapping from the pharmacy, and she made a big fuss for Christopher's sake. Then, when she saw the diamond watch, she could hardly believe her eyes.

I really got her for once.

CONKS I celebrated Christmas in Buffalo, and at a family gathering, I mentioned something about how tough it was to play with a broken thumb for a couple of weeks.

"Yeah," my cousin, Kris Ann Piazza, said, "try living with a broken neck for seven years."

She's going to start college in September, in her wheelchair. She's an amazing girl.

SIMMS I watched the wild-card game between the Rams and the Redskins, and I wanted the Rams to win. I thought they had a chance if they pressured Jay Schroeder into some mistakes—it was his first playoff game—but they didn't, and that killed them, that and Eric Dickerson's fumbles. Nothing personal against the Redskins. I just wanted the Rams to win because I preferred to play them the following week instead of the 49ers.

As soon as the game ended, I started thinking about the 49ers, worrying about their aggressive, complicated defense. We beat them in the playoffs in 1985, and they beat us in 1984, the year they went on to win the Super Bowl. They won the Super Bowl two years before that, too. The 49ers made me nervous.

I couldn't wait to go work out the next day and get it out of my system.

Parcells began abusing the offensive line as soon as he knew we were playing San Francisco. He started calling them "Club Thirteen" because Joe Morris ran thirteen times against the 49ers the last time we played them and gained only 14 yards. He loves to have a weapon he can use to motivate the linemen, to get them pissed at him, to make them kill themselves to show him up. He knows how to motivate. But actually, Parcells should've called them "Club Fourteen" because he was upset by the number of yards, not the number of carries.

Coach Parcells started our work week the same way he started every work week during the regular season. He told us who we were playing. He told us we were playing San Francisco. Most of us knew that already. He told us who might be hurt for them and who might be coming back, and he told us, in general terms, what we had to do to beat them.

He also told us to be careful with the media.

He's always telling us to be careful with the media. He'd

like us never to say one bad word about our opponents, and never say one good word about ourselves. We come close.

We went out on the field two hours early to beat the snow that was predicted. Lionel Manuel practiced for the first time in three months.

CONKS The Associated Press named Lawrence Taylor the Most Valuable Player in the National Football League, the first defensive player to be selected in fifteen years, since Alan Page of the Minnesota Vikings.

The AP also named Bill Parcells the NFL Coach of the Year. Everbody needled Parcells. "Getting too many stars around here?" I asked him.

Everybody congratulated Lawrence.

He may not be the best athlete on the team, but he's certainly the baddest.

SIMMS Ron Erhardt found something in the 49er films. "Look at this," he told me. "We got some good stuff." He showed me what seemed to be a flaw in the San Franciso pass defense, a weakness we could exploit by running a certain pattern. We looked at the films over and over, and the more we saw, the more certain we were we could take advantage of them. "It's unbelievable," I said. "It's got to work."

Almost every week, when you watch the films, you find something, not always something that good, but always something. But the question is, when you find something and you try to exploit it, how quickly will they adjust?

John Iacono/Sports Illustrated

Wide World

Both Phils, McConkey (*left*) and Simms, got
carried away in the Super Bowl—McConkey by
tight end Mark Bavaro after scoring a touchdown,
Simms by tackle Brad Benson after passing for a
touchdown—and neither the passer nor the
receiver came down to earth for several weeks.

Denver's John Elway (*above, left*) was the superstar of the Super Bowl—until the game began. Then McConkey (*left*), encouraging the crowd, and Simms (*below*), encouraging the officials, took command.

Bob Grieser/Los Angeles Times

Perfectly protected in a perfect pocket, Simms (*above*) passed perfectly in the first quarter of the Super Bowl, seven throws, seven completions. In the third quarter, McConkey reached the brink of perfection, but knew he was upended short of the end zone (*right*) by just that much.

Wide World

Patrick Downs/Los Angeles Times

Paul Bereswill/Newsday

Simms burned the Broncos on the ground (*above*) and in the air (*left*). He ran three times and gained 25 yards, passed 25 times and completed 22 for 268 yards. He set Super Bowl records by completing 88 percent of his passes and by completing 10 in a row.

The ball was headed for Bavaro's
hands (*right*), but bounced loose
(*below*) until McConkey grabbed
it just before it hit the ground
(*bottom*) for the touchdown he had
always dreamed of.

McConkey (*left*) and Simms (*above*) had their hands and heads up all through Super Bowl XXI. It was, for each, the greatest day of his career.

Everybody wanted to pat Simms on the backside after the most precise passing performance in Super Bowl history.

Who's the only man who played for the Giants in the Super Bowl who wasn't in the team photo? It wasn't McConkey (*second row from top, second from left*) or Simms (*front row*). It was Tom Flynn.

Among the other spoils of the Super Bowl: Simms and McConkey joined a flock of stars to flex their muscles for an exercise video.

1987

In which McConkey and Simms put
on Super Bowl performances that
match their wildest dreams

SIMMS I wasn't used to driving from my home to Giants Stadium without a lot of traffic, but on New Year's Day the road
was wide open, and I guess I was so surprised, I started
speeding. The next thing I knew, a cop pulled me over. I
showed him my registration, and he said, "Where's your li-
cense?"

"At home," I said.

"That's a good place for it," he said.

I was positive he was going to give me a ticket till he said,
"What's your last name?"

"Simms," I said.

"What's your first name?"

"Phil."

"You play football?" he said.

"Yes, sir."

The officer kind of laughed and put away his pen. "Could
you just slow down a little, Mr. Simms?" he said.

"Yes, sir," I said.
"Good luck Sunday," he said.
"You too, sir," I said.

Two days before the first playoff game, I lifted weights. I always lift on Friday. I don't care if my arm is a little tired on Sunday. In fact, I want it to be. I want the ball to feel a little heavy.

Sometimes the worst thing that can happen in a game is for you to have a real live arm, because then you have a tendency to overthrow. I've heard baseball pitchers say that when their arm is really live, they lose a little control. I know it's a fine line, but I'd rather my arm be a little tired. That's one of the reasons I warm up hard before a game.

I want my body to be tired, too. I don't want to get a good night's sleep the night before a game. I stay up late, watch a movie, maybe two movies, anything that's on, it doesn't make any difference. I want to get a few hours' sleep and wake up feeling kind of tired. Then I'll drink maybe two or three cups of coffee and eat some toast to get me going. I like to feel a little goofy before a game. I play better when I do.

CONKS The day before we played the 49ers, Washington beat the defending Super Bowl champions, the Chicago Bears, to advance to the National Conference championship game, and Cleveland beat the New York Jets to advance to the American Conference championship game. We were kind of looking forward to getting another shot at the Bears—they eliminated us the year before—but the Redskins spoiled that plan.

SIMMS We reactivated Lionel Manuel the day before the San Francisco game. He missed the last twelve games of the regular season, and I missed him. I had a special relationship with Lionel. I trusted him more than I trusted any other receiver. I trusted him to get open and I trusted him to catch the ball.

I trusted the other wide receivers, too, but not the way I trusted Lionel. Of course I trusted the tight end. You have to trust that guy. I'd never met anyone like Bavaro. Very intelligent. Very religious. And very, very tough.

He went back to Notre Dame during the summer of '86, and I heard he got hooked up with some mind guru. "What'd you study?" I asked him, and Mark said, "How to use your mind to be oblivious to pain."

"That sounds appropriate," I said.

I don't think Bavaro knows what pain is.

I've got a pretty high threshold of pain myself. A quarterback had better. If you can't play hurt, you're not going to play a whole lot. My theory is that no matter what they do to me, I'm not coming out, no way. I missed too many games in '81 and '82 and '83. I never missed one since, and just as long as I can stand up, I'm not going to.

Parcells gave us our usual Saturday-night speech at the Woodcliff Lakes Hilton, which is where we spend the night before home games. He told us we were better than the 49ers. He also told us that the crowd would be on our side. Nothing fiery. Nothing unexpected. We all knew what was at stake.

Ray Perkins used to give us a speech almost every day, and some were tremendous, and some were just weird. He told us a story once about a guy who broke his kneecaps in a car accident. They fixed him up, but his knees were fused, locked so that he had to walk very stiffly. The guy was determined to get flexibility back in his knees, so one day he put heavy weights on his feet to hold them in place, leaned forward and then threw himself back as hard as he could, and his knees cracked right at the joints. From then on, Perkins said, he was able to walk normally. "Men," Perkins said, "if you want something bad enough, you can get it!"

By ten o'clock, after our team meeting, I was in my room. I always room alone. It's a tradition with quarterbacks. I watched TV till after midnight, went to sleep and woke up at four-thirty in the morning and couldn't get back to sleep. I took two showers, and I still couldn't fall asleep. I knew I was going to be a little goofy for the 49ers.

CONKS Before the start of the 49ers game, I jumped up on our bench and began twirling a towel, stirring up the crowd. The crowd got into it. I kept it up during the game. I guess it was like John Madden said. The crowd could identify with me and my enthusiasm. I wasn't putting it on. It was my style. If I hadn't been in uniform, I might've been in the crowd, cheering louder than anyone else.

SIMMS The third play of the game, Michael Carter, their nose tackle, broke through and belted me in the mouth as I threw a pass behind McConkey. I said to myself, "Well, I guess it's gonna be that kind of day." I wasn't surprised. I knew they were good pass-rushers.

CONKS The first time they got the ball, the 49ers almost scored. Montana completed three passes in a row, and the third was a slant-in to Jerry Rice, who suddenly broke into the clear and seemed to be on his way to a touchdown. But at our 26-yard line, in the open, without being touched, Rice dropped the ball. He tried to pick it up, but couldn't, and the ball rolled all the way to the end zone.

Kenny Hill recovered for us, and we promptly drove 80 yards for a touchdown. Joe Morris got half those yards on five running plays, and Simms ended the drive with a pass to Bavaro for a touchdown.

Halfway through the second quarter, after a San Francisco field goal, Morris broke off tackle for 45 yards and a touchdown and a 14–3 lead. That gave Joe more than 100 yards rushing with more than half the game to go.

The blocking on the touchdown run was beautiful. The offensive line was responding pretty well to Parcells's "Club Thirteen" needling.

SIMMS We were at the San Francisco 28-yard line, fourth down and six to go, two minutes left in the first half. It was still a close game. A field goal—from 46 yards out—would've given us a fourteen-point lead, good, but not great. Parcells, who used to be so conservative, decided, as he did so often in 1986, to gamble.

We lined up in field goal formation, but then Jeff Rutledge, the holder, called, "Shift," and Jeff moved into the shotgun. Raul Allegre, the kicker, became a flanker, and the 49ers were so confused they covered Allegre, who couldn't catch the ball even in practice, and let Bavaro go free. Rutledge passed to Mark for a first down at the 5-yard line.

After a holding penalty, we had third and goal at the 15 with less than a minute till halftime. We sent Bobby Johnson toward the right corner of the end zone, hoping to exploit the weakness Ron Erhardt had spotted in the films. I held the ball as long as I could. Then, as I threw, Dwaine Board, a defensive end, hammered into me, bowled me over. My head pounded against the ground. I never saw the play. I barely heard it.

My chin was cut. My mind was fuzzy. As I came off the field, Burt spotted the blank look on my face and told me it was a touchdown. Pat Hodgson told me it was a hell of a pass. Later, when I looked at the tape, I saw that it was a good play, well conceived and well executed. There was nothing lucky about it. The only thing that wasn't planned was the welt on my face.

Bavaro was really worried about me. "You okay, Phil?" he asked me. "You sure you're all right? Are you sure?" It was the longest conversation I ever had with Mark.

Two plays later, while I was sitting on the bench, still trying to get my head back together, I heard screaming and yelling and I saw guys jumping up on the bench to get a better view. I managed to see Lawrence Taylor running into the end zone to give us a 28–3 halftime lead. I didn't see him intercept Montana's pass, and I didn't see Burt crash into Montana as he released the pass, sending him sprawling, slamming his head against the ground just as mine had been slammed a few minutes earlier. But I was fortunate. I was just dizzy. Montana had a concussion. His season was over.

CONKS Six minutes into the third quarter, Simms sent me down the right sideline on a fly pattern, and he threw a perfect pass, leading me into the end zone, and the ball floated into my arms, and I had a playoff touchdown. It was Simms's third touchdown pass of the game, and we were ahead 35–3.

SIMMS When Conks scored, I knew the game was over. I knew there was no way in the world they could score five touchdowns on our defense in less than twenty-five minutes. A few minutes later, I threw my fourth touchdown pass, to Zeke Mowatt, and then Joe Morris ran for his second touchdown, and with three touchdowns in less than nine minutes, we had an unbelievable 49–3 lead, and we were still in the third quarter.

I got a sore back in the fourth quarter.

From sitting on the sidelines.

CONKS While Simms was sitting on the bench in the fourth quarter, catching his breath, I stood up behind him and turned to the crowd and pointed to him and led the fans in cheers. Damn, he deserved it.

I'd been there enough times when he'd been booed, and now he'd thrown four touchdown passes, which was a playoff record for the Giants, and he'd earned the cheers. He was my hero. He was as big as Jack Kemp once was to me.

Strangely, when Montana went down, it was Jeff Kemp, Jack's son, who took Joe's place at quarterback for the 49ers.

SIMMS As we watched the clock wind down in the scoreless fourth quarter, I turned to Brad Benson and said, "For once, we don't have to pace the sidelines at the end and just pray that the defense can stop 'em."

CONKS We had won ten of our regular-season victories by a combined total of forty-four points. Now we had won one game by forty-six points, the third greatest margin in NFL playoff history.

After the game, several of the guys were talking about Simms. "A lot of quarterbacks will duck or throw it away," Jim Burt said. "Phil stood in there, and that's why he's a great quarterback. When the guy's barreling down on him, and Phil knows he's gonna get it, that's when he makes the great plays."

L.T. said the same thing more succinctly. "He's a cocky son of a bitch," Lawrence said. "That's what makes him such a great player."

SIMMS Parcells would've loved to have heard me with the reporters after the game. I told them I thought we had a pretty good team and I thought I played a pretty good game. When they asked me about the Redskins, I said, "It's fitting that the two best teams in the conference will meet in the championship game. It'll be a good game. It'll be physical."

I really opened up. I was asked about my relationship now with the fans, and I said I didn't know. I was asked why we played so much better against the 49ers this time, and I said I didn't know. I also didn't know if we played a perfect game —and didn't know if Rice's drop set the tone for the game. I even said I didn't know how many games in a row we'd won.

Nobody believed that one. But I really didn't. I'm terrible with numbers.

I only slipped once. "What about the people who say the Giants are just defense and Joe Morris?" somebody asked, and I told him where the experts could shove those theories.

"I'm tired of hearing that," I admitted.

CONKS My mother watched the 49ers game on television in J.J.'s Lounge with Bob Curran, a columnist for the *Buffalo Evening News*. She told Curran that, at Giants Stadium, she would rather sit with the regular fans than with the wives of the other players. "They spend too much time talking about their family situations," she said, "and don't pay enough attention to the game to suit me. And I don't feel like turning around and telling the wife of some big star to keep quiet so we can concentrate on the game."

SIMMS I told people I was sorry Montana got hurt, and at first I think I was just saying it because I was supposed to. But after a while, I began thinking about it, and I really did feel bad. I also felt a little guilty.

I had bad feelings toward Montana before the game—I just didn't like him—and I realized afterward that I really didn't know him, certainly not well enough to judge him. People judge me without knowing me, and it bothers the hell out of me, and here I was doing the same thing with Montana.

Burt wasn't happy about hurting Montana, either. Burt's had his own back problems, so he could identify with Montana.

I couldn't wait to get home to watch the tape of the game. But when I turned on my VCR, the tape was blank. Diana had set the recorder wrong. I had to borrow a neighbor's copy.

*　*　*

My dad called me after watching the 49ers game on TV. "Well, son," he said, "they can't deny it anymore. Damn, you're one of the best! And you're the toughest son of a bitch that ever stood back there. I'm just so proud of you, son, I had to tell you."

It was better than being named MVP in the Pro Bowl. It was even better than hearing it from Parcells or Lawrence or Benson. Dad had never praised me like that before. We finished talking and I hung up and I just sat there for a minute and then I called out, "Diana!" She came over to me and I said, "You'll never believe what my dad said to me."

I told her, and she said, "That's nice. That's so nice."

I was just floating.

The morning after the 49ers game, McConkey and I walked into the weight room just after Parcells left. Chris Godfrey and Karl Nelson and Bart Oates, three of our offensive linemen, were lifting, and Johnny Parker turned to Godfrey and said, "Well, Chris, you gonna tell Phil what Coach told you?"

Chris kind of turned red. What happened was that, a few minutes earlier, Parcells had stuck his head in the door and said, "If I was you guys, I wouldn't be so proud right now." He had told them he thought the offensive line did a miserable job of protecting me from the 49ers. "My quarterback took too many shots in the mouth," Parcells had said.

I wasn't surprised at what he'd said, but, of course, I never would've yelled at those guys myself. My mouth was too sore for me to yell.

CONKS They were replaying the 49ers game in the trainer's room, and I kept ducking out of the weight room to watch it. "I don't know why you want to go in there and watch," Johnny Parker said to me. "You only made one play."

I also returned seven punts, which tied the NFL playoff record.

SIMMS Chris Godfrey tried to strike up a conversation with Mark Bavaro in the weight room the next day. "Mark, I hear you're getting married," Chris said.

Mark said, "Yeah."

"Is it gonna be after the season's over?" Chris asked.

Mark said, "Yeah."

"Have you got your honeymoon set?"

Mark said, "No."

"Are you taking her to Hawaii for the Pro Bowl?"

"Yeah."

"Is that gonna be your honeymoon?"

"No."

You see, when you talk to Mark, he's got short answers and long answers. "No" is his short answer. "Yeah" is the long one.

CONKS "You know what I just realized?" I said to Simms after we lifted.

"What?"

"The girl I'm gonna marry is probably only nine years old right now."

That'd make her twenty-one when I'm forty-one.

That sounded about right.

SIMMS Fishof and I ate lunch at Il Villagio, an Italian restaurant not far from the stadium, and as we were getting into the pasta, a customer walked over to our table and said, "I want you to know, I never booed. I don't know why they booed you, but I never did."

He probably didn't.

"Thank you," I said.

David told me I'd be receiving a bonus from the Giants because we won the division and I'd get another bonus if we won the conference championship. "Really?" I said.

"Yeah," David said. "It's right in the contract."

"You sure?" I said.

"I swear."

"Golly, I hope so."

I really had no idea. I'd never read the fine print in the contract, that's David's job.

We were just finishing our meal when another customer stopped and said, "You guys are the greatest. I just bought my wife a new diamond ring on account of the money I made on the 49ers game. You guys are the greatest."

I guess when you're winning, everybody gets bonuses.

Parcells didn't just pick on the offensive line. He was cutting everyone. He said he heard that "Good Morning America" had an interview with Carl Banks. "Can you imagine waking up to that face?" Parcells said.

He had words for McConkey, too. "He's Z-100 now," Coach said. "Pretty soon he'll be Z-50, then Z-25 and then Z-nothing."

CONKS The City of New York and the city of Moonachie, New Jersey, started dueling over us. Ed Koch, the mayor of New York, said at first there was no way the city would throw a ticker-tape parade for us, the way they did for the Mets, because we were a foreign team, a New Jersey team, not a New York team, and he didn't want to waste the city's money on us. Then American Express offered to pay the bill for the parade, and somebody told the mayor that a lot of Giants fans voted in New York City. He said he might reconsider his decision. Meanwhile, the mayor of Moonachie, which is close to Giants Stadium, promised us the greatest parade in the history of his town if we chose Moonachie over Manhattan.

SIMMS We had our first workout for the Washington game on Wednesday, and afterward there must've been nine million reporters in the locker room. I never saw so many. It was horrible.

I stayed in the weight room. Conks didn't get there till 4:35. That's because the reporters were kicked out at 4:30.

CONKS There must've been nine million reporters in the locker room. I never saw so many. It was wonderful.

We knew the Redskins would give us a tough game, but it was hard not to look ahead to the Super Bowl. Guys were already worrying about getting enough tickets for the game, and getting their families out to California, and I was already seeing myself making a diving catch for a touchdown in the Rose Bowl.

I don't think the Redskins were looking beyond us.

Dexter Manley wasn't talking to the press at all, not a word, and Benson made it a point to keep telling the media how much he respected Manley, what a good clean player he thought Dexter was. Brad didn't want to give Manley any more incentive than he already had.

SIMMS By Friday night, less than forty-eight hours before we were going to play the Redskins, I was good and sick. I knew it was coming. Christopher came down with the flu Tuesday, Deirdre started showing symptoms on Wednesday and I began feeling lousy Thursday.

Then, on Friday, after we practiced in cold, ugly weather, Carl Banks and I were taken into New York by helicopter to talk at a news conference. Reporters kept asking about the effect of the weather, and I told them that in Giants Stadium the big problem was the wind, not rain or snow. Parcells had a better answer. He said he was hoping it would snow when they had the ball and be sunny when we had it.

Someone asked me if I was thinking about playing in my first Super Bowl, and I told them I'd already played in a bunch of Super Bowls. "While I'm driving back and forth to work," I said.

The helicopter took us back to New Jersey and I went home and went to bed.

CONKS Everybody talks about Parcells's superstitions, how he collects elephants with their trunks up, and how he won't pick up a penny unless it's heads up, but I think I spotted one that no one else noticed. He always comes out to practice wearing gray sweats with the initials B.P. on them, and sneakers and socks, and he always has the right pant leg rolled up. No matter how cold it gets, he always shows some skin on his right leg. It's got to be another one of his superstitions.

SIMMS I went to the stadium Saturday morning, and it was raining so hard we didn't go outside. I watched films for a while, got home after eleven and went to bed and slept till six-thirty. Then I got up, showered, went to the Woodcliff Lakes Hilton, sat through the meetings, went to my room, drank some chicken soup and went to bed. Ronnie Barnes gave me something to help me sleep, and I had a ton of orange juice in my room. Every time I woke up during the night, I drank a glass of orange juice and then went back to sleep. By the time I got up for breakfast, I'd slept about sixteen or seventeen hours since Saturday morning.

I really wasn't worried. I knew my adrenaline would get me through the game. I drove over to the stadium and I was surprised because the wind wasn't too bad. I figured it would die down by game time, the way it usually does.

This time it didn't.

CONKS Two hours before the kickoff, an hour before the full team started loosening up, I went out on the field to jog and stretch. I always go out early, and when I come back in to the locker room, Simms always asks me about the wind. When he asked me this time, all I could do was roll my eyes.

While we were loosening up, John Elway led Denver on a five-minute 98-yard touchdown drive that tied up the game in the closing seconds in Cleveland. The Broncos beat the Browns for the American Conference championship in overtime.

SIMMS By game time, the wind was blowing around twenty miles an hour and gusting up to more than thirty. It was the worst I'd ever seen in Giants Stadium.

CONKS The first critical play of the game was the coin toss, and we were outnumbered. They had seven captains at the center of the field. We had Harry Carson. Carson won. Russ Grimm called tails for them, and the coin came up heads.

SIMMS It was a good thing Harry didn't have to make the call. We never would have won. He's one of the worst callers in history.

CONKS We took the wind at our back for the first quarter, and we let Washington receive the kickoff, hoping we could pin them deep in their own territory, and the strategy worked perfectly. Allegre kicked the ball through the end zone. They couldn't move, and then Steve Cox got off a punt into the wind that went only 23 yards and out of bounds.

We got the ball at the Redskins' 47-yard line, and a few plays later, Allegre kicked a 47-yard field goal that gave us a 3–0 lead. Even with the wind, it was a hell of a kick.

Again, Allegre's kickoff was too deep to return. Again, the Redskins got nowhere in three plays, and again they punted.

This time, we got possession at the Washington 38. On third and twenty at the Redskins' 36, Simms hit Lionel Manuel for 25 yards and a first down. Lionel made a good catch—his first in four months.

Three plays later, Simms threw to Bobby Johnson for a touchdown, and when that play was called back because of a motion penalty, Simms threw to Lionel for a touchdown. Lionel ad-libbed on the touchdown. He just kept moving around till he was open.

We were ahead, 10–0, less than ten minutes into the game.

SIMMS Washington got the wind in the second quarter, but it didn't do them any good. Halfway through the period, we were on their 9-yard line, second down and two to go. I went up to the line of scrimmage planning to audible, to call a pitch to Joe Morris going left.

My head said *left,* but my mouth said *right.* I called the numbers for a pitch to the right. I took the snap, and, naturally, everybody went right—except me. I was still thinking left. I turned to pitch the ball, and I was all alone. My first thought was to fall down, but there was nobody anywhere near me. It would've been too embarrassing. So I ran for the end zone. I got all the way to the one-yard line. I would've scored if I hadn't been so startled.

Curtis Jordan, their free safety, said to me later, "Damn, you did it to us again." I'd run some good bootlegs against them in the past.

"Curtis," I said, "it wasn't planned."

"Don't even say that," he said.

"I blew the play," I said.

He was more angry than if I'd done it on purpose.

Joe Morris scored on the next play, and we had a 17–0 lead, and for all practical purposes, the game was over. I took the rest of the game off. I was seven-for-ten in the first quarter, then only threw four harmless incomplete passes the rest of the game. Hand off. Hand off. Hand off. Joe took all the punishment, twenty-nine carries. I wasn't even sore.

CONKS With less than two minutes to go before the half, Steve Cox punted with the wind and I caught the ball at our 27-yard line. I moved forward 5 yards, and then Reggie Branch, a 227-pound running back, one of their special teams players, just came flying into me at full speed. It was a spectacular hit—you could hear it in the stands—and half the people in the stadium, I guess, thought I was dead. I wasn't even wounded. I leaped right up, fired my fist in the air, maybe shook it just a little toward Branch's face, to let him know he hadn't fazed me, then raced off the field, feeling terrific. The crowd loved it.

I caught six punts in the swirling wind at Giants Stadium and, no matter how hard the Redskins hit me, no matter how hard they tried to strip me, I held onto the ball. Parcells said afterward it was the best job I'd ever done, and Al Davis, the owner of the Raiders, said it was the best job he'd ever seen of punt-catching.

It made up for the fact that my streak of consecutive games of catching at least one pass ended at seven. I was only 125 games short of the NFL record.

It's no accident that I've never fumbled a punt away—not in high school or college or the NFL. I practice catching punts every day. I practice and practice and practice. I start by just throwing the ball straight up, a nice spiral. Then I watch it fall. It's easy to follow the ball until it gets just above your head. The hard part is from there to just below eye level. Your eyes have to anticipate the descent of the ball. Most balls are lost in that eight- or ten-inch span from the top of your head to the bottom.

Once I've got my eyes tuned up, I like to practice catching the ball with my fingertips just before it hits the ground. Good hands are important, but not as important as good eyes. I've got tiny hands—and perfect eyes, pilot's eyesight.

I also practice catching more than one ball at a time—one that's punted to me and one that I throw up in the air. I concentrate absolutely. I don't hear the crowd. I don't hear footsteps. I don't hear anything. It's just me and the ball. One of the Dallas coaches once said, "McConkey could catch a punt in a rock slide."

SIMMS "I'll bet you five hundred I get a sack," Dexter Manley offered Benson during the first half, and by late in the second, Dexter knew he had lost the bet. "It's not fair," he told Brad. "The bet shouldn't count. You guys stopped throwing in the first half."

Benson was generous. "I'll settle for a beer at the Pro Bowl," he told Manley.

CONKS The game ended, 17–0, which meant that we had won our two playoff games by a combined score of 66–3 and our last four games by a combined margin of 114 points. We were even hotter than the Bears had been going into Super Bowl XX.

The Redskins probably never had a more futile day. They were zero-for-fourteen on third-down conversions, zero-for-four on fourth-down conversions. They gained a total of only 190 yards running and passing, even though Jay Schroeder threw fifty passes. He was sacked four times.

Parcells and Carson dueled on the sidelines. Parcells came armed this time. After Harry dumped the Gatorade on him, Parcells shot back with a water pistol. The Gatorade ritual had gotten a little tiresome for the players, but it had become such a big thing for the public that, on CBS, John Madden diagrammed and analyzed the play. Waiting for the shower probably kept a lot of people from tuning out, because the game itself was over early.

The Giants announced at the end of the game that, win or lose in the Super Bowl, a celebration would be held two days later, on January 27, in Giants Stadium. The mayors of New York City and Moonachie, New Jersey, both lost out.

SIMMS At the end, the field was littered with confetti, and rolls of toilet paper and shredded newspapers swirled in the air, mingling with the cheers and shouts of fans celebrating as they had not celebrated in thirty years. No one seemed to notice the cold and the darkness. The Giants were going to the Super Bowl.

Jim Burt was so fired up he managed to scale the ten-foot-tall blue wall circling the field. He climbed into the stands and began wading through delirious Giant fans, yelling and waving to everyone as he worked his way toward his wife, Colleen.

The fans went crazy, welcoming Burt, embracing him, but two people were upset. Parcells was one. He was upset because he was afraid Burt might get hurt. "Somebody could've stuck a knife in you," he told Jim later.

But Parcells was only mildly annoyed. McConkey was really annoyed. He was pissed because Burt hadn't told him that he was going into the stands, hadn't invited him to come along.

McConkey hated seeing Burt get all that attention alone.

I told the reporters I was thrilled about going to the Super Bowl, but I wasn't thrilled about facing Denver again. I remembered how terrific their pass defense was. I remembered how complicated it was.

I also remembered to say all the right things about John Elway.

CONKS I went out and partied, and somewhere, sometime in the middle of the night, after I'd fallen in love several times, I told a desperate young woman from "Good Morning America'' that I'd stay up all night and do the show in the morning. I couldn't go to sleep anyway, I was so excited. I was going to the Super Bowl, and I wasn't dreaming. It wasn't a fantasy anymore. I was really going to the Super Bowl.

I appeared on "Good Morning America," and my mother appeared on "Good Morning Buffalo." She'd been out partying, too.

SIMMS I celebrated by going home and taking care of Diana. She'd fought off the flu as long as she could, but, finally, Saturday night, after she sent me off to the hotel, she'd come down sick. She missed the game Sunday, the first home game she'd missed in years. I was supposed to go on the "Today" show Monday morning, but I had to cancel. I had to stay home to help Diana and the kids.

I didn't mind at all. She had taken care of two sick kids and a sick husband all week, and she had let me keep my mind completely on the game.

I was just sorry she hadn't been there at the stadium to hear all the cheers. She had heard enough boos and enough cussing over the years.

CONKS Parcells was delighted we were playing Denver, because it gave him ammunition to use against the offense. He reminded "The Suburbanites" and Simms and Joe Morris and me and anyone else who wandered close to the weight room the day after the Washington game that the offense hadn't scored a touchdown when we played the Broncos during the regular season.

SIMMS Parcells gave us three days off after the Redskins game, just enough for Fishof to start taking advantage of all the offers that were coming in. Jim Burt, Joe Morris and I posed for a poster that Adidas wanted to get out right away.

They had us all wearing sunglasses, but only Joe looked like he belonged in them. Jim McMahon doesn't have to worry. Burt and I just don't make it in shades.

We went back to Fishof's office after the shoot, and when David told us that Gatorade wasn't interested in a commercial with the Giants—they said they wanted people to drink Gatorade, not to pour it all over each other—Burt said he had a terrific idea.

"What's that?" Fishof said.

"Let's go to Pepsi or to Coke," Burt said. "Tell 'em we'll pour their stuff on Parcells. The hell with Gatorade."

David lit up. He said he'd look into it. He also said he had offers for me to go on the Joan Rivers show a few days before the Super Bowl, or the Carson show a few days after. David said if I wanted to do Carson, I couldn't do Joan Rivers first. I said I'd rather wait until after the game and do Carson, and Burt and McConkey immediately volunteered to take my place on Joan Rivers. Burt got the booking.

We started practicing for the Super Bowl ten days before the game, on Thursday, January 15. Parcells brought us back to reality quickly. After a tough ninety-minute closed practice, he has us run eight 100-yard sprints.

"Simon Legree found his whip," Kenny Hill said.

"Parcells is losing his mind," Burt suggested. "He's gone haywire."

I enjoyed the practice. I was over the flu, and I had the feeling right from the start that I was going to have a good game against the Broncos.

We each got twenty-five tickets, at $75 apiece, for the Super Bowl. I needed all of them, and more. I'd invited my mother and father and all my brothers and sisters and their husbands and wives to come out to California for the game. I also had friends I had to take care of. It was a good thing that several guys on the team owed me favors.

CONKS I started writing a Super Bowl column for the *New York Post* nine days before the game, and in my first column I had an exclusive. I revealed that Mark Bavaro ate shredded wheat with skim milk for breakfast. I also revealed that he ate breakfast with me, sitting on a trunk in the rehab room.

Five of my teammates were also doing columns. "Can any of them write?" Parcells asked the regular newspapermen.

SIMMS Conks wasn't taking any chances. He was writing for the *Post* and doing a commercial for the *Daily News* and he probably would've delivered the *New York Times* if they had asked him.

Parcells didn't let up on him. "When you guys leave here Sunday," Parcells told us in a team meeting, "you get on the bus and you go straight to the runway. You don't go through the terminal. There will be a press tent set up near the plane, but you don't have to go over to it. It's mostly for the photographers who want to cover our departure."

Parcells paused. "But you can go there if you want, Mc-Conkey," he said, "and you'll have time to do four or five interviews. Congratulations, McConkey. You've moved up to number one. You've passed Burt. You're the number-one self-promoter on the team now."

CONKS Our second Super Bowl practice, which was just as brutal as the first, ended with eight 60-yard dashes. It looked like we were getting ready for the Olympics. "Our focus is not so much on the Super Bowl," said Kenny Hill, the only guy on our team with a Super Bowl ring, "as it is on getting through practice alive."

Simms had another sensational workout. "Phil was phenomenal," Bart Oates said. "He hit everything he threw. He has this strange sort of glow, like he's in a perfect biorhythm or something."

Even Parcells was impressed. "Hey, this is too much," he yelled at Simms. "Save something for the game."

SIMMS The day before we left for California, Parcells told me, he received three elephants with their trunks up. He couldn't have been happier if he had received the Denver playbook. I wouldn't say the man is superstitious, but he changed our chartered plane from a 727 to a DC-10, which probably cost an extra ten or twenty thousand, because he wanted to have a pilot named Augie Stascio, who'd flown two winning Super Bowl teams in the past and only flew DC-10s.

CONKS The first crisis came at the airport, before we took off in the snow to fly from Newark to Long Beach, California. Because the bus took us straight to the plane on the runway, Bavaro and I weren't able to purchase our usual ration of pistachio nuts in the terminal. Mark always buys the red. I always buy the plain. He insists they taste different. I tell him they're just colored differently. When I give him a blind taste test, he can't tell the difference. Mark really seemed disturbed by the fact we couldn't buy any pistachio nuts. Fortunately, Pat Hodgson had pistachio nuts with him, and even though he doesn't coach the tight ends, he gave some to Mark and calmed him down.

The second crisis came a few minutes later, in the air. The weather was bad and the visibility low, and after we took off, the pilot raised and lowered the landing gear to try to get the ice off it. When he lowered the gear, it made a strange sound, and a few of the guys got a little tense. "What happens if the plane goes down?" somebody wanted to know. "Does Denver win the Super Bowl automatically, or do they send the Redskins in our place?"

SIMMS They showed two movies on the flight out to California —*Tough Guys* and *Karate Kid II*. You think Parcells was trying to tell us something?

CONKS Jim McMahon of the Bears got in trouble at Super Bowl XX because somebody quoted him as saying that all the women in New Orleans were sluts. I think Landeta *hoped* all the women in Southern California were. He and I and Simms had dinner our first night in Costa Mesa, and Landeta, as usual, had only one thing on his mind. He left us at dinner because he said he had to get back to the hotel to meet his *dates*. Just as Simms and I returned to the South Coast Plaza, a car pulled up next to us, and two knockout blondes got out. We parked, and as we walked into the hotel, our suspicions were confirmed. Landeta was walking through the lobby with one on each arm. I don't know how his leg holds up.

SIMMS Bruce Willis left a message for me on tape at WPLJ, the radio station I moonlight for. "Phil, you are the baddest," he said. One thing about playing for the New York Giants— we do have some pretty well-known fans.

CONKS Bobby Johnson, who'd been fighting a cold, was so filled up with Coricidin that in between our morning meeting and our first workout at Rams Park in Anaheim, he fell asleep on the floor of the locker room. He didn't get much rest. There was a large retriever roaming around the locker room, and Lawrence Taylor found a rubber ball and began playing catch with the dog. Then L.T. put the ball on Bobby's chest. A few seconds later, the retriever landed on the receiver, and Bobby ran a "go" through the locker room.

The rest of us got to do our sprinting later, six 80-yard dashes at the end of a practice that had to be one of the three or four hardest of the year.

Parcells might've had a mutiny on his hands—if we weren't getting ready for the Super Bowl.

SIMMS You can't believe how good it felt to throw a football in warm weather. I was able to grip the ball better than I had gripped it in months. I could make it do anything I wanted. I could throw hard or soft, short or long, it didn't make any difference. The ball carried beautifully. The receivers kept shaking their heads.

I was excited by the way I was throwing, and I was excited by the game plan. We wanted to surprise them. We were going to come out throwing, and we were going to keep on throwing. I couldn't have been happier.

The newspapers and the magazines made it sound as if the game was just going to be played between John Elway and Lawrence Taylor, scrambling and rambling, but that was okay with me. That was fine. I wanted to sneak up on them.

CONKS We put in some time on a fleaflicker, a trick play that we hadn't used, even though it had been in our playbook all year. The play was designed to cross up the opposition when they got preoccupied with stopping Joe Morris. It was simple: Simms pitched out to Morris, who faked a run, then lateraled to Simms, who threw a long pass downfield to one of the wideouts. Bobby Johnson and I had practiced the play for weeks, and I knew it was going to work against Denver, either to Bobby or me.

SIMMS David Fishof called to tell me that the Disney people wanted to do a commercial with the Most Valuable Player in the Super Bowl as he walked off the field at the end of the game. "You want to do it?" David said.

"Forget it," I said. "I'll never be the MVP. They don't go for quarterbacks."

Only three quarterbacks had won the award in the previous fourteen years—Terry Bradshaw twice, Joe Montana twice and Jim Plunkett once. "No way I'm going to win," I said.

David is devoutly opposed to turning down a possible commission. "I'll tell 'em to forget about the MVPs," he said. "I'll tell 'em to make it the quarterbacks."

"I don't know, David," I said. "I don't know about doing it right on the field."

"Don't worry," he said. "The game's over. You only do it if you win. Nobody's going to care what you do then. It'll be fun. It'll be okay. It'll pay good. Trust me."

The funny thing is, I trust David.

CONKS Tuesday was the traditional "photo day." We all put on our uniforms and scattered around the football field at Orange Coast College, just a mile or so from our hotel, and then they let the media loose to take our pictures and talk to us. I heard there were 2,500 media people out for the Super Bowl, which meant there were about fifty-five for each Giant. I know I had my share.

"We're just doing this for Phil McConkey," Brad Benson said on television. "It has nothing to do with the rest of the New York Giants. It's just Phil McConkey Day."

"Was it an honor to be traded for an eleventh-round draft choice?" one reporter asked me.

"Honor, schmonor," I said. "I don't care how I got here. I don't care if I got here through the sewer tunnels, as long as I got here."

Most of the questions were better than that one, and I didn't mind holding court for about an hour. Bavaro and Morris didn't talk to the media at all. Somebody had to make up for them.

SIMMS After the photo session, Parcells gave us the day off, and Burt, Benson, Godfrey, Oates and a few other guys went deep-sea fishing. Most of the guys caught fish. Burt caught a sea gull. Lawrence played golf. I was supposed to play with him—I could've used the cash—but I decided I'd have all spring to play golf. I didn't want to tire myself out. So I went and lifted weights instead. Conks and I got Johnny Parker to find us a place where we could lift. I wouldn't have felt right if I hadn't lifted.

CONKS After we lifted, I went to dinner with Vince Ferragamo, who interviewed me for a radio show he was doing. I hadn't seen him since Green Bay. He told me that he told his three daughters I was playing in the Super Bowl. "Is he bringing us candy?" they wanted to know.

SIMMS While Conks ate with Ferragamo, I just had room service and watched Vince and O. J. Simpson in "First and Ten," that HBO show which is sort of like "Dallas" with shoulder pads. It's a football soap opera. It's so bad I think it's good.

Conks and Burt and Fishof and I stayed up late to watch Burt on the Joan Rivers show, which he had taped just a few hours earlier. Naturally, she asked him about the Gatorade. "It's like when you're kids," Burt said. "You know, everybody picks on the fat kid."
The studio audience laughed.
"He'll torture you for that one," I told Burt.
"Oh, he ain't watching this," Burt said.
"Somebody'll tell him," I promised.

CONKS We went out to stretch before practice at Rams Park and as always, I was in the front row, on the right side, second from the end. Harry Carson and Lee Rouson were on my left, as always, and O. J. Anderson on my right. Harry was yelling across me at Ottis. "He was drowning in the ocean," Carson said, "and we threw him a life preserver. Now he's in the love boat."
In 1975, when Ottis was a freshman at Miami and I was a plebe at Navy, our teams met in a regular-season game in the

Orange Bowl. In 1979, when I was an ensign and Ottis was a rookie with the Cardinals, he rushed for more than 1,600 yards, an NFL record for rookies. We had certainly taken different routes from the Orange Bowl to the Super.

Parcells stood between me and Ottis while we stretched—the field is Johnny Parker's domain during calisthenics, but Parcells, of course, can go wherever he wants, whenever he wants—and looked at me and said, "You know, you ought to pay me a finder's fee. For finding you in Green Bay. If I hadn't found you, you know what you'd be doing right now? You'd be freezing your ass off, selling snowblowers in some little town in Wisconsin. You owe me."

I did.

SIMMS I told our receivers that the Super Bowl was a challenge—to them and to me. I told them everybody said we couldn't throw—not against Denver, anyway. I told them nobody gave us credit. I told them they weren't supposed to be fast enough or big enough or elusive enough.

I told them we were going to prove everyone wrong.

CONKS All year long, we'd heard that the wideouts were the weak underbelly of the team, but I knew we had five tough SOBs who could go over the middle and catch the ball in a crowd, who could get our heads knocked off and our helmets cracked and still get back up. We might be slow and ugly, like Pat Hodgson always told us, but under pressure, in the Super Bowl, I'd take us over a bunch of world-class, pretty-boy wideouts every time.

The Broncos said we were going to get hit like we'd never been hit before.

I couldn't wait.

SIMMS I was surprised how comfortable I felt with all the media hype. Usually, I'm not too eager to do interviews—in the first place, I always try to watch what I say, and in the second, I get tired of hearing myself—but I didn't mind at all at the Super Bowl. I was available for just about everybody.

Monday night, I was one of a handful of players who sat with Parcells and answered questions, and after that, I met Len Berman and Bill Mazer in the hotel lobby and did interviews with them for New York television. On Tuesday I went through "photo day," and on Wednesday and Thursday I had two more long sessions with the media, and I actually enjoyed it. I always had an army of cameras and notebooks around me, and I pretty much said what I felt—within limits. I wasn't going to give the Broncos any ammunition.

"When you think of the Denver Broncos, you think of John Elway," I said. "When you think of the New York Giants, you don't think of Phil Simms, you think of Lawrence Taylor." That was my theme song, and I played variations on it all week. I talked about the importance of Joe Morris and our defense, and I didn't even hint that I might be throwing a lot more than usual. I was cooperative, but I was careful.

I just made up my mind that I was going to enjoy the hype and I was going to enjoy the game, and I wasn't going to let anything bother me. I'd been through enough bad times. I was going to enjoy the good times.

The only thing that was going to bother me was if the game didn't turn out right.

■ Lawrence Taylor wanted to be in bed. Mark Bavaro wanted to be alone. But most of the New York Giants seemed to enjoy, or at least tolerate, the mass sessions with the media that preceded the Super Bowl.

Pepper Johnson, the rookie linebacker, cheerfully explained that he got his nickname from his childhood love for spicing his foods. He said he used to put pepper on his cereal. He said he still puts pepper on his pie.

"You put pepper on cake and pie?" said Tony Kornheiser of the *Washington Post*.

Johnson looked at Kornheiser as if he had asked the dumbest question in the world. "Not cake, man," he said. "Pie."

Carl Banks, another youthful linebacker, said that at the age of four, he spent three years in prison. "I murdered an aunt," he said. "With a horseshoe." Grilled by the press, Banks eventually confessed to not commiting the murder. "I was just trying to entertain you guys," Banks said.

Jim Burt tried to entertain, too. He told reporters that his back-up, Erik Howard, the rookie nose tackle from Washington State, often sat in a corner and talked to his plant. Burt made up the story about Erik and the stalk. "It's tough coming up with new material," the veteran admitted.

Burt had no trouble coming up with Sean Landeta material. "We've got some guys who blow-dry their hair," he said. "They don't play defense, and they don't play offense. Let's leave it at that."

Bart Oates, the center, talked about Parcells's tag for the offensive line, The Suburbanites. "That's us," he said. "A wife, a family life, small kids, a grill in the backyard. We made Simms an honorary member. He's a family man in the suburbs. He lives in a really ritzy part of town, but I think we can overlook that."

Kenny Hill, the defensive back, put a bottle on his interview table with a sign: "Kenny Hill Fine Relief Fund—All Contributions Accepted." After two days, he had $1.04, only $4,998.96 short of the $5,000 Hill acknowledged he had been fined by Pete Rozelle, the commissioner of the National Football League. The fine was for aggressive acts Hill aimed at wide receiver Jerry Rice of the 49ers in the Giants' opening playoff game.

Hill, who majored in molecular biophysics at Yale, sought to explain his tendency to be physical on the football field, a tendency intensified during his years with the Oakland and Los Angeles Raiders. "We are expected to go through a mental metamorphosis," Hill said, "to go from being gentlemanly and following the rules of society to people who play violently and aggressively for two or three hours on Sunday. It causes us to do things out of character. We have to be able to call upon these tendencies on demand and three hours later submerge them on demand."

Bavaro opted for brevity. He did reveal he had broken his jaw against New Orleans early in the season. "Did it hurt your talking?" he was asked.

"Not that anyone noticed," Bavaro said.

"What do you like about football?" someone said.

"It's a job," Bavaro said.

"A job you like?"

"For two or three years, it's a living," he said. "When it's over, I'll find something else to do."

"What do you want to do then?"

"That's personal."

Lawrence Taylor was more belligerent. "I don't want to be here," he said, "but I'm here. They said I had to do it. It's NFL policy." Taylor said he was very tired. He was asked why. "I went out until three A.M.," L.T. said. "I went to a prayer meeting."

Taylor suggested that the reporters, too, had stayed up late, thinking of stupid questions. "When you get sick, start yelling and your eyes start turning red, when you feel like slapping your mama, you're ready," L.T. said. He meant for the game, not for the interview session.

SIMMS Three days before the Super Bowl, at our final mass session with the media, Mike Lupica of the New York *Daily News* said to me, "Phil, have you thought about what's gonna happen if you guys lose?"

"Well, Mike," I said, "I don't really think about that."

"You know all the writers and all the people in New York are gonna blame it on you," he said. "No matter how the game goes, no matter how many points you score, they're still gonna blame it on you."

Out loud, I said, "Well, I haven't thought of it that way."

To myself, I said, *I don't give a damn if they do blame me. I'm gonna play my same old way.*

I really didn't give a damn. I wasn't scared about messing up in a Super Bowl. Suppose I did, what could they do to me? Write something bad about me? Boo me? Say bad things about me in front of my family? I'd been through all that crap so many times, it didn't frighten me.

I think I was finally ready to be a success.

I was ready to win a big one.

CONKS I didn't fall asleep in any of the meetings, but some of the guys did. I didn't blame them. Two weeks was just too long a time to get ready for a game. Everything became monotonous, repetitious. How many times could you watch the same film? I stayed awake, but I didn't pay attention. I kept fantasizing, seeing the same thing I'd been seeing for twenty years, seeing myself making a diving catch for a touchdown in the Super Bowl.

The wives and children and families flew in Thursday— after their plane sat on the ground in Newark for four hours because of bad weather. My mother and father were on the charter. They got divorced a couple of years after I finished college, but they still saw each other, they still talked, and they didn't mind sharing the suite I got them the night before the flight at the Sheraton across the street from Giants Stadium. I had a limousine take them to and from the hotel. I got a kick out of spoiling them. They'd spoiled me when it was a lot tougher for them.

My sister Debbie flew in from Dallas with her husband Bill,

who's a computer wizard and a sports nut, and Kit McCulley and his new wife Susan flew in from Pensacola. They were all in on the dream when it started in 1983, and now they all wanted to see how it came out. I was just sorry that Hank and Glo George couldn't make the trip.

SIMMS Diana left Deirdre home in New Jersey with a babysitter, but she brought Christopher with her to California. He was full of energy after the plane ride. He came running down the hall of the Westin South Coast Plaza shouting, "Daddy! Daddy! Guess what? Mark Bavaro said hi to me!"

Fishof was delighted. He called to tell me that the Disney people had agreed to use the quarterbacks, Elway and me, in their commercial after the Super Bowl game. "When the game ends," David said, "they'll come up to you with a camera, and they'll ask you where you're going now, and all you have to do is say, 'I'm going to Disney World.' "

"That's all?" I said.

"Well, you have to do it twice," David said. "You also have to say, 'I'm going to Disneyland.' They need one version for the East Coast and one for the West."

"How do I find them after the game?"

"They'll be using NFL Films," David said. "They'll find you. Remember, only if you win. You get paid either way, win or lose, but you only have to do it if you win. I mean, *when* you win."

David was getting all excited. He was staying in Beverly Hills, and he was having meetings all day long, about me, about the Monkees, the musical group he represents, about everything. Only they don't say they *have* meetings in Beverly Hills. They say they *take* meetings. David told me he took three lunches one day.

CONKS At our final workout at Rams Park, we ran through our two-minute drill, the hurry-up offense we use in the closing minutes of a game or a half, and Simms completed six out of six passes to six different receivers. He never threw better.

After practice, we moved to our base for the last two nights before the Super Bowl, the Beverly Garland Hotel in North Hollywood, right next to the freeway leading to the Rose Bowl.

We were within striking distance.

SIMMS The night we moved up to the Beverly Garland, Mc-Conkey and I went out to dinner with Billy Crystal, the co-median. I knew he was funny—I'd seen him on "Saturday Night Live"—but I didn't know he knew so much about sports. He told me he grew up cheering for the Giants, for Tittle and Gifford and Robustelli and Rote.

He asked intelligent questions, so I figured the least I could do was give him intelligent answers. He asked me about the game plan, and I told him we were planning to pass a lot more than usual, and he asked me if we already knew our first series of plays, and I told him we knew the first play, a pass that was supposed to go to Lionel Manuel, and I outlined it for him on the table with the salt and pepper shakers.

"Can I bet the guy next to me in the Rose Bowl twenty-five dollars that that's going to be the first play?" he said.

"You can bet on it," I said.

He said he was surprised we didn't use the option pass with Joe Morris, because of the way the defense moves up on him, and I told him the problem was that Joe had trouble throwing the ball because he has such small hands, but that we did have a play in which I flipped the ball to Joe and he lateraled it back to me and then I threw a pass.

McConkey butted in and said, "Yeah, and I'll cut across from right to left, and I'll be wide open." Billy laughed. He thought we were kidding.

CONKS My old roommate, John Mistler, who'd been out of pro football for two years, stopped by the Beverly Garland to say hello, to wish us luck. I know he would have loved to have been part of it. I dreamed about the Super Bowl more than most guys, but still it's every player's dream.

Parcells got Mistler tickets for the game. Parcells is like that. He takes care of his former players, which makes the current players feel good, too, because we know we're all going to be former players someday.

I think Parcells picked that up from Al Davis and the Raiders. He really respects Al Davis and he tries to emulate him in many ways.

My family stopped by to see me, too. So did Connie McQuestion's mother and sister and brother. Connie was still in Buffalo, but her family had moved to California.

SIMMS We were supposed to have a final walk-through practice at the Rose Bowl the day before the game, but we talked Parcells out of it. It wasn't hard. We reminded him that the day before we played the Cowboys in Dallas in our opening game, we went to their stadium—and we lost. We reminded him that the day before we played the Raiders in Los Angeles and the 49ers in San Francisco, we didn't go to their stadiums —and we won. "Why mess with something that works?" Andy Headen said, and Parcells agreed with him.

CONKS The night before the Super Bowl, Simms and Bavaro and I went to see the movie *Platoon*. It certainly put the game in perspective. I thought about the MIAs and the POWs, and I wondered how many were still in Vietnam, maybe not even knowing that the war was over.

If I ever had to go into combat, I wouldn't mind having Simms on one side of me and Bavaro on the other.

I slept for about three hours that night. I woke up for good at a quarter after four. I wished the game was going to start at dawn.

I lay in bed and kept imagining myself making big plays. I knew we were going to run the fleaflicker, and I knew I'd be in for it, and I knew it would be a big play. I kept seeing myself cut across the field, catch the ball from Simms and go in for a touchdown. It was beautiful. I didn't want to sleep.

I was twenty minutes early for Mass. I couldn't wait for it to start, either.

At the pregame meal, I couldn't eat much, just Product 19 and some corn flakes. Then Bavaro, Nelson and I took a cab to the Rose Bowl.

Mark didn't say a word. But neither did Karl or I.

We got to the Rose Bowl about four hours before game time. We were ready for the kickoff.

SIMMS I felt so good warming up in the Rose Bowl. "Nervous?" Benson asked me.

"No," I said. "Not nervous. Excited. I feel great. I'm gonna be throwing some fastballs today. Give me time and I'll rip 'em."

I coasted. I went at half speed. I had such good rhythm I didn't want to mess with it.

CONKS DREAMS ARE ONLY FANTASY FOR AS LONG AS IT TAKES TO MAKE THEM REALITY.

The words were crocheted in blue lettering on a white background, Giant colors, with a red border. My uniform number —80—was crocheted under the words.

I put the gift in my locker in the Rose Bowl, stood it up so that I could read the message. My mother brought it from Buffalo for me. It was crocheted by my cousin, Kris Ann. It took her seventy-two hours to make it, holding the hook in her teeth.

SIMMS I couldn't miss. The first time we got the ball, after they scored on a field goal, I completed five straight passes. I threw the first one on first down to Lionel Manuel, for 17 yards, just the play I'd diagrammed for Billy Crystal. I hope he made the bet.

I threw the fifth one to Zeke Mowatt for 6 yards and a touchdown and a 7–3 lead.

CONKS It was fitting that Zeke Mowatt should score our first touchdown in the Super Bowl. He was so typical of our guys. He was a free agent who came to the Giants in 1983, the same year I tried out. He came from Florida State, where he was used mainly as a blocker and rarely as a receiver. When he came to training camp, there were two veterans and two high draft choices ahead of him at tight end, but he worked so hard improving his pass-catching, and his blocking was so awesome, he beat out Gary Shirk and Tom Mullady and the two rookies and became the starting tight end.

Zeke was good as a rookie. He was sensational in 1984. He should've been named to the Pro Bowl. Then, in training camp in 1985, he ripped up his knee and sat out the whole season. But he worked as hard as anyone on the active roster. He was in the stadium every day, strengthening his knee, stretching it, enduring incredible pain to break the surgical adhesions. It hurt me just to watch him. Most people would have quit, would have said there was no way to come back from knee surgery like that. But Zeke just pushed himself further, drove himself beyond reasonable limits, that free-agent mentality. He came back in 1986, almost as good as ever. Sure, he was frustrated, playing behind Bavaro—you don't want guys on your team who don't think they ought to be playing—but, again, he didn't quit, he didn't bitch, he didn't grumble. he worked even harder.

It all paid off with his Super Bowl touchdown.

SIMMS Elway couldn't miss, either. In the first quarter, I was seven-for-seven, and he was six-for-six. Late in the period, he ran 4 yards for a touchdown that put them in front, 10–7.

CONKS They had a chance to put us deep in a hole in the second quarter, but they didn't do it. They had first and goal on our one-yard line, on the brink of a ten-point lead, and in three plays they lost 5 yards. Then Rich Karlis missed a 23-yard field goal attempt.

A few minutes later, Karlis had another easy shot, from 34 yards, and he missed that one, too, and Denver was in trouble. Just before the half, we pinned them deep in their own territory, and George Martin broke through and grabbed John Elway—who had tried, and failed, to tackle George the first time we played them—and threw him to the ground in the end zone for a safety. That seemed to shake up Elway, who had completed eleven of his first thirteen passes, literally and figuratively.

We went to the locker room at halftime, trailing only 10–9 and feeling that we were in control, that they had the lead, but we had the strength, the skill and the momentum.

As we trotted back on the field for the second half, the loudspeaker was blaring and Sinatra was singing "New York, New York." I flew down the sidelines, whirling my arms, waving my towel, and between me and Sinatra, we got the crowd roaring. I was pumped. I was as high as a human being can be.

SIMMS Jeff Rutledge came through under pressure again. The first time we got the ball in the second half, we came up short of a first down on our own 46-yard line. Fourth down and barely a yard to go, a perfect place to play safe in a Super Bowl. We didn't.

We lined up in punt formation, then shifted, and Jeff went under the center and delayed the count, hoping to draw the Broncos offside. He waited as long as he could, looked at Parcells, who nodded, and then took the snap and drove straight ahead for more than the yard we needed for the first down.

Five plays later, I spotted Bavaro in the end zone, in double coverage. I probably shouldn't have thrown the ball, but I saw a small opening. The ball snuck through, and we went ahead, 16–10.

CONKS I saved my longest punt return of the year for the Super Bowl, a 25-yard return that took us inside the Denver 35-yard line, set up a short field goal for Allegre and gave us a 19–10 lead.

Tom Flynn, who'd started the season with me in Green Bay, ended it with me in the Super Bowl. Tom broke a bone in his left wrist on my punt return, but he had already done his share. He was in on all three tackles on our first three kickoffs.

I'd told Parcells that Flynn could tackle.

With a minute to go in the third quarter, our ball, second-and-six on the Denver 45-yard line, Ron Erhardt, up in the press box, told Pat Hodgson, on the sidelines, to call the fleaflicker. Hodgson got so excited, he turned to me and said, "Zero-slot, weak, Z-motion, toss, one-thirty-five—"

"*Four*-thirty-five, dammit!" Parcells said. "*Four*-thirty-five!"

I sprinted to the huddle. I knew the play was going to work. I knew either Bobby Johnson or I was going to make a big gain. I was so excited I couldn't get the play out to Simms. I was almost stuttering. "Uh, zero, uh, weak, uh, uh," I said. "Oh shit, the fleaflicker!"

Simms was perfectly calm. He's always calm, but I'd never seen him this calm. He knew what I meant. "Zero-slot, weak, Z-motion, toss, four-thirty-five, fleaflicker," he said, and the huddle broke, and Bobby Johnson and I both split out to the left. Then I went in motion to the right, to Bavaro's side.

As soon as the ball was snapped, I checked to see if the strong safety was blitzing. If he blitzed, I had to block him.

He didn't. I hesitated—a thousand and one, a thousand and two—as if it were a running play, moved downfield a few yards, then cut to my left at a forty-five-degree angle.

Simms tossed the ball back to Morris, who headed for the line of scrimmage, and the Denver defense reacted exactly as we had hoped it would, anticipating a running play.

As I cut across the field, I saw Steve Foley, the free safety, move up, and then I saw his eyes widen, and I knew that Joe had spun and lateraled the ball back to Simms. Now Foley knew it was going to be a pass, and he was double-clutching desperately, trying to get back in position, too late. I was past him. I was wide open. So was Bobby.

Simms hit me in stride as I crossed the Denver 20-yard line. I looked the ball in, turned my head upfield and all I could see was green grass and white stripes, and I said, "Lord, You're going to let me score a touchdown in the Super Bowl." I was positive I was about to score a Super Bowl touchdown.

Then I saw Mark Haynes, setting himself in front of the goal line, between me and a touchdown, my former teammate, the man who had complimented me for my tackling when I was a rookie. I considered cutting back to my right, but Foley was coming up behind me, and someone else was coming from the right, and I thought one of them might catch me around the five.

I decided to just go straight for the goal line, get as much as I could, try somehow to get past Haynes. He went low, and I went high. I tried to go over him, but he flipped me, and when I landed, I knew I hadn't scored. I knew I was on the one-foot line.

I rolled into the end zone, leaped up and threw my arms in the air, then fell down, actually bawling, and pounded the ground, frustrated by coming so close to my dream, so close to scoring in the Super Bowl.

Joe Morris ran the ball in on the next play, and we had a 26–10 lead.

SIMMS I thought the fleaflicker just ended the game. When McConkey went down to the one, that was it, it was over. It was a great call, and I didn't even hit the right guy. Bobby Johnson was wide open for a touchdown, and I didn't even see him.

CONKS We got the ball back a few minutes later, early in the fourth quarter, on Elvis Patterson's interception of a John Elway pass, and we moved quickly toward the Denver end zone, third-and-goal on the 6-yard line. Simms called the play, 63 divide, a slant, Bavaro cutting from left to right, over the middle. The play developed perfectly, and Simms fired a strike, slipping the ball past the Denver defenders, hitting Mark's hands just as he soared past the goal line.

I don't know why Mark didn't catch the ball. Ninety-nine times out of a hundred, he would've. But this time the ball ricocheted off his hands, flipped end over end and sank toward the real turf of the Rose Bowl.

I was trailing Mark into the middle, and as the ball flew loose, I dove. I dove the way I dove into parked cars and snowbanks in Buffalo. I dove the way I dove against Army, the way I dove in my first mini-camp, the way I dove in so many dreams.

I caught the ball just before it hit the ground.

I cradled it. I caressed it.

I leaped into Bavaro's arms, thrust the ball high as he held me, and I saw the biggest smile on Mark's face.

Mark never smiles when he scores a touchdown.

He looked at me. "I take care of my buddies," Bavaro said.

I skipped off the field with the ball, handed it to Ed Wagner, the equipment manager, and told him to take it to Fort Knox, to lock it away.

The ball I caught was the last one Simms threw in the game. It was his tenth straight completion. It gave him twenty-two completions in twenty-five attempts, with three touchdowns and no interceptions. No quarterback—not Starr, not Namath, not Staubach, not Bradshaw, not anybody–ever came so close to perfection in a Super Bowl.

I looked up into the stands, trying to spot my parents, in section 17, row 45, wanting to share the moment with them. I thought of all the great players who had never scored a touchdown in the Super Bowl, thought of all the great players who had never even played in a Super Bowl, players like Kemp and Gilchrist and Dubenion and Butkus and Karras and O. J. Simpson.

I thought of all the sacrifices I had made, the weights I had lifted, the sprints I had run, the parties I had passed up, and I knew it was all worth it.

We were going to win the Super Bowl. I was experiencing the greatest high known to man.

SIMMS We won, 39–20, and for once, even I loved the sound of the statistics.

I completed twenty-two of twenty-five passes, 88 percent, breaking the Super Bowl record of 73.5 percent, set by Ken Anderson.

I completed ten straight passes in the second half, breaking the record of eight, shared by Joe Theismann and Lenny Dawson.

I was named the Most Valuable Player in Super Bowl XXI.

I turned on the sidelines and I hugged McConkey.

CONKS With two minutes left on the clock, Benson and Oates gave Simms his first shower of the season, pure ice water. Thirty seconds later, Parcells got his seventeenth, from Carson, pure Gatorade.

SIMMS As I walked off the field, a cameraman came running up to me, aimed his lens in my face and cued me for the Disney commercial. "I'm going to Disney World," I said.

Then, for the West Coast audience, I said, "I'm going to Disneyland."

They didn't have to tell me to smile.

CONKS Pepper Johnson and William Roberts stood on the 50-yard line and did a disco dance they had learned as undergraduates at Ohio State. Jim Burt and I ran around the field and mingled with friends and fans. Liza Minnelli sang, "New York, New York," on the public-address system, and Burt and I sang along with her. We had rhythm, the kind you would expect from two white guys from Buffalo.

■ "This should put an end to all that talk about Phil Simms not being a great quarterback," Bill Parcells said.

SIMMS It was close to perfect, it really was. I didn't throw one ball where I said, "Damn! I want that one back!" Maybe one. The last touchdown pass. I threw it too hard. I threw it so hard Mark couldn't catch it.

CONKS You can't have that one back.

My mother and father came to the victory party at the South Coast Plaza, and they were in heaven. They both said it was the greatest day of their lives. My father even told me I played a good game. My mother talked to everyone and posed for pictures with everybody from Lawrence Taylor to Tom Cruise. My father, puffing on his long brown cigarettes, made an impression in his own quiet way. "Man, that's the kind of guy I want on my side if I'm in a fight," Leonard Marshall said.

Tom Cruise and I talked about the navy, about pilots I knew from the Naval Academy and he knew from *Top Gun*, former Navy football players. He's a fan; he wore a Giants hat, and his mother wore a Simms jersey. He told me that

224

working with Paul Newman in *The Color of Money* had gotten him interested in auto racing.

I wonder what I'm going to do when I stop playing football, when I grow up. I know I may never play another down in the National Football League. I know I may get cut before the 1987 season. I know the Giants are going to bring some rookie wide receivers to training camp who are bigger than me and faster than me and younger than me, and I know that every one of them is going to be looking for my job. What if one of them takes it? What do I do then?

Why can't I be a race driver?

Why can't I be an actor?

Why can't I be anything I want to be?

I can. I know if I want something badly enough, and I work hard enough, I can get it. The Super Bowl proved that.

I don't know exactly what I'll do when football's over, but I know it'll be something with a certain degree of risk and excitement. I need that.

I enjoyed meeting Tom Cruise, but the most impressive person I met at the party was a child, an eight-year-old boy named Michael Gillick. He was dying from cancer of the nervous system. He wasn't supposed to make it past the age of two. He was a Giants fan from Toms River, New Jersey, and a few weeks before the game, he'd said if he could see us win the Super Bowl, he could die in peace. A state senator from New Jersey named Russo and an organization called Make A Wish worked together to make Michael's wish come true.

Michael's face was distorted, puffed up, one eye almost shut. He looked like somebody had hit him with a baseball bat for three days. But he was beautiful. He was intelligent, articulate, cheerful, full of life. He had more charisma than Tom Cruise, more than anyone I'd ever seen. When I met him and held him and hugged him, I liked him instantly. I liked him as much as anyone I'd ever met. Maybe more.

I wish I had his courage.

* * *

At four o'clock in the morning, Simms, Burt, Banks, Carson and I hooked up in the lobby and did the "Today" show for NBC. Then Phil, Harry and I did "The CBS Morning News." We finished at four-thirty. "C'mon, Conks," Simms said. "Let's go get something to eat."

"Okay," I said. "Where we going to go?"

"We'll jump in a cab," Simms said. "The driver'll know where to go to eat."

We got a cab, and the driver took us to a hotel in Irvine that had an all-night restaurant. It was five in the morning. *USA Today* was already out, and so was the *Los Angeles Times*. Half the front page of the sports section of the *Times* was a picture of me, throwing my arms up in the air after my first catch. Underneath my picture was a much smaller picture of Simms and L.T.

I looked at the menu, but I couldn't read anything. Simms ordered bacon and eggs. I don't eat bacon and eggs. Too much fat. Too much cholesterol. "I'll have the same," I said.

We ate. We looked at the papers. We didn't say much.

Then at one point I looked at Simms and I suddenly realized that he was the Super Bowl MVP, that he had just had the greatest Super Bowl of any quarterback in history and that he was sitting with me eating bacon and eggs.

I thought about Starr and Namath and Staubach and Bradshaw, all the great heroes of other Super Bowls, and I tried to put Simms in their class, I tried to think of him as a hero.

I couldn't.

He's my friend. I watch him get his shoulder rubbed every day. We sit in the steam and shoot the shit every day. We cut each other down all the time. I couldn't put him up on some pedestal.

The sun was coming up after the best day of my life, and he was just Phil to me.

■ A few weeks after their Super Bowl breakfast, Phil Simms and Phil McConkey shared a dinner at a small unpretentious

basement restaurant in East Harlem that serves unbelievable Italian food to such customers as Robert Redford and
Woody Allen and Jerry Lewis and Claus von Bulow and
Martina Navratilova, none of whom ever creates much of a
stir.

Simms and McConkey created a stir.

One customer climbed off his bar stool, went to his car,
drove home to New Jersey, picked up his son and a neighbor's son, and drove back to get autographs from Simms and
McConkey. The host and the bartender asked to pose for
pictures with Simms and McConkey. They were, for the moment, the hottest celebrities in New York.

Everybody wanted them for appearances or commercials. They went to California together and shot an exercise
video. Simms went to Atlantic City and roasted Jim Burt.
McConkey went to upstate New York and endorsed Jack
Kemp. Simms went to Louisville to the Kentucky Derby
kickoff luncheon and told them how he used to scale the
fence to sneak into the Derby. McConkey went to a Sports
Illustrated luncheon and met the stars of the annual bathing-
suit issue.

McConkey stepped up in league. He hung out with Keith
Hernandez of the Mets, a heavyweight bachelor. He dated a
Penthouse Pet and a former Miss New York State and a former Miss Michigan, and Simms said, "Yeah, Conks won't
go out with a girl any more unless her first name is 'Miss.' "
But McConkey still had his moral code—and a fear of in-
fection. After one date, he confessed, "We just did some of
what used to be called 'heavy petting,' but is now called
'safe sex.' "

In March, four months before training camp was to begin,
Simms and McConkey went back to heavy workouts, back to
four days a week in the weight room, back to stretching and
strengthening with Johnny Parker. When they slipped away
for a few days to shoot their video in California, Parcells
taunted them, "Oh, we're still training just as hard as ever, is

that it, only now we're doing it in California?'' But the truth was they were training as hard as ever. Simms turned down far more commercial opportunities than he accepted. McConkey turned down far more social opportunities than he accepted.

The Giants—players and management—felt that the Chicago Bears had succumbed to too many post–Super Bowl temptations, had sacrificed their hunger and their cohesiveness, and they didn't want the same thing to happen to them. The NFL urged the Giants, as Super Bowl champions, to play a preseason exhibition in London, as the Bears had done the previous year, but the Giants refused, left the championship of England to be contested by the Denver Broncos and the Los Angeles Rams. The Giants feared that a week in London would disrupt their training schedule and their psyches, would distract them from their goal of becoming the first team to win back-to-back Super Bowls in the 1980s.

The Giants are favored to repeat. They are a young team, their average age in the Super Bowl under 26, with young stars rising, Eric Dorsey coming up fast behind George Martin, Erik Howard emerging behind Jim Burt, Pepper Johnson primed to replace Harry Carson. Johnson, who wears a gold jalapeño pepper around his neck, is so talented some teammates commit the heresy of saying that if he is not already better than Lawrence Taylor, he soon will be.

In the college draft, in April 1987, the Giants chose three wide receivers in the first four rounds. Their first-round selection—the first wide receiver ever drafted by the Giants in the first round—was Mark Ingram of Michigan State, a wideout whose skills are expected to delight Phil Simms and to challenge Phil McConkey.

McConkey knows there is no guarantee that he will be a New York Giant in the fall of 1987. He knows that the three wide receivers chosen in the early rounds of the draft are looking to chase him to another team or to another line of work. He knows they can take away his job.

But they can't take away what he did on January 25, 1987.

Super Bowl XXI.

Simms to McConkey.

Touchdown.

Dear Phil

Dear Phil:

Congratulations on a great victory and a great TD catch on behalf of the old Buffalo Bills you watched in the '60s, including Kemp, Dubenion, Gilchrist and all. We are proud of you. You watched us as a young boy in War Memorial Stadium, and I was privileged to see you win Super Bowl XXI with my family. Tell Jim Burt we're proud of him as well and hope to see you in person soon to say America needs more Phil McConkeys. All the best to you and the Giants.

> *Your friend,*
> *Jack Kemp*
> *Member of Congress*

Dear Phil:

I just want to congratulate you on a tremendous season and great Super Bowl. I went to the game with mixed emotions because of my great respect for Dan Reeves and the job he's done in Denver. But I also had an allegiance to the Giants because of my feelings toward a fellow Naval Academy graduate like you and also my link with Billy Belichick. Phil, again you have done a great job on and off the field. I wish you the best for continued success.

> *Sincerely,*
> *Roger Staubach*

P.S. You have really made us former USNAers proud. Way to go, #80. Roger.

Statistics

PHIL SIMMS

Regular Season

PASSING

Year	Att.	Comp.	Pct.	Yards	TDs	Int.	Long	Rating
1979	265	134	50.6	1,743	13	14	61	65.9
1980	402	193	48.0	2,321	15	19	58t	58.9
1981	316	172	54.4	2,031	11	9	80	74.2
1982	—	—	—	—	—	—	—	—
1983	13	7	53.8	130	0	1	36	56.6
1984	533	286	53.7	4,044	22	18	65t	78.1
1985	495	275	55.6	3,829	22	20	70t	78.6
1986	468	259	55.3	3,487	21	22	49	74.6
Totals	2492	1326	53.2	17,585	104	103	80	73.9

RUSHING

Year	Attempts	Yards	Average	Long	TDs
1979	29	166	5.7	27	1
1980	36	190	5.3	20	1
1981	19	42	2.2	24	0
1982	—	—	—	—	—
1983	—	—	—	—	—
1984	42	162	3.9	21	0
1985	37	132	3.6	28	0
1986	43	72	1.7	18	1
Totals	206	764	3.7	28	3

PHIL SIMMS
Post-Season

PASSING

Year	Att.	Comp.	Pct.	Yards	TDs	Int.
1984						
Los Angeles	31	22	71.0	179	0	0
San Francisco	44	25	56.8	218	0	2
1985						
San Francisco	31	15	48.4	181	2	1
Chicago	35	14	40.0	209	0	0
1986						
San Francisco	19	9	47.4	136	4	0
Washington	14	7	50.0	90	1	0
Denver	25	22	88.0	268	3	0
Totals	199	114	57.3	1,281	10	3

RUSHING

Year	Attempts	Yards	Average
1984			
Los Angeles	4	−1	−0.3
San Francisco	1	3	3.0
1985			
San Francisco	5	−5	−1.0
Chicago	—	—	—
1986			
San Francisco	1	15	15.0
Washington	7	−2	−0.3
Denver	3	25	8.3
Totals	21	35	1.7

STATISTICS

PHIL McCONKEY
Regular Season

PASS RECEIVING

Year	No.	Yards	Average	Long	TDs
1984	8	154	19.3	39	0*
1985	25	404	16.2	48	1
1986	16	279	17.4	46	1
Totals	49	837	17.1	48	2*

* One touchdown scored on fumble recovery

PUNT RETURNS

Year	No.	FC	Yards	Average	Long	TDs
1984	46	15	306	6.7	31	0
1985	53	18	442	8.3	37	0
1986	32	12	253	7.9	22	0
Totals	131	45	1,001	7.6	37	0

KICKOFF RETURNS

Year	No.	Yards	Average	Long	TDs
1984	28	541	19.3	33	0
1985	12	234	19.5	43	0
1986	24	471	19.6	27	0
Totals	64	1,246	19.5	43	0

PHIL McCONKEY
Post-Season

PASS RECEIVING

Year	No.	Yards	Average	Long	TDs
1984					
Injured	—	—	—	—	—
1985					
San Francisco	0	0	0	0	0
Chicago	1	23	23	23	0
1986					
San Francisco	1	28	28	28t	1
Washington	0	0	0	0	0
Denver	2	50	25	44	1
Totals	4	101	25.3	44	2

1986–1987 Game-by-Game Results

Date	Result	NYG		Opp.	Record
Sept. 8	L	28	at Dallas	31	0–1
Sept. 14	W	20	San Diego	7	1–1
Sept. 21	W	14	at L.A. Raiders	9	2–1
Sept. 28	W	20	New Orleans	17	3–1
Oct. 5	W	13	at St. Louis	6	4–1
Oct. 12	W	35	Philadelphia	3	5–1
Oct. 19	L	12	at Seattle	17	5–2
Oct. 27	W	27	Washington	20	6–2
Nov. 2	W	17	Dallas	14	7–2
Nov. 9	W	17	at Philadelphia	14	8–2
Nov. 16	W	22	at Minnesota	20	9–2
Nov. 23	W	19	Denver	16	10–2
Dec. 1	W	21	at San Francisco	17	11–2
Dec. 7	W	24	at Washington	14	12–2
Dec. 14	W	27	St. Louis	7	13–2
Dec. 20	W	55	Green Bay	24	14–2
NFC Divisional Playoffs					
Jan. 4	W	49	San Francisco	3	15–2
NFC Conference Championship					
Jan. 11	W	17	Washington	0	16–2
Super Bowl XXI					
Jan. 25	W	39	Denver (at Pasadena)	20	17–2

Super Bowl XXI

SCORING

	1st	2nd	3rd	4th	Total
NEW YORK GIANTS	7	2	17	13	39
DENVER BRONCOS	10	0	0	10	20

DEN—FG Karlis 48
NYG—Mowatt 6 pass from Simms (Allegre kick)
DEN—Elway 4 run (Karlis kick)
NYG—Safety Elway tackled by Martin
NYG—Bavaro 13 pass from Simms (Allegre kick)
NYG—FG Allegre 21
NYG—Morris 1 run (Allegre kick)
NYG—McConkey 6 pass from Simms (Allegre kick)
DEN—FG Karlis 29
NYG—Anderson 2 run (kick failed)
DEN—V. Johnson 53 pass from Elway (Karlis kick)

Field goals missed—Karlis 2 (24, 34)

Attendance—101, 063

TEAM STATISTICS

	NYG	DEN
First downs	24	23
by rushing	10	5
by passing	13	16
by penalty	1	2
Rushes, yards	38–136	19–52
Net yards passing	263	320
Sacks, yards lost	1–5	4–32
Passes completed, thrown	22–25	26–41
Interceptions, yards returned	1–(−7)	0–0
Plays, net yardage	64–399	64–372
Punts, average	3–46	2–41
Punts returned, yards	1–25	1–9
Kickoffs returned, yards	4–53	5–84
Fumbles, lost	0–0	2–0
Penalties, yards	6–48	4–28
Time of possession	34:39	25:21

INDIVIDUAL STATISTICS

RUSHING

Denver	Attempts	Yards	Average	TDs
Elway	6	27	4.5	1
Wilhite	4	19	4.8	0
Sewell	3	4	1.3	0
Lang	2	2	1.0	0
Winder	4	0	0.0	0
Totals	19	52	2.7	1

New York	Attempts	Yards	Average	TDs
Morris	20	67	3.4	1
Simms	3	25	8.3	0
Rouson	3	22	7.3	0
Galbreath	4	17	4.3	0
Carthon	3	4	1.3	0
Anderson	2	1	0.5	1
Rutledge	3	0	0.0	0
Totals	38	136	3.6	2

S I M M S   T O   M c C O N K E Y

PASSING

Denver	Att.	Comp.	Pct.	Yards	TDs	Int.
Elway	37	22	59.5	304	1	1
Kubiak	4	4	100.0	48	0	0
Totals	41	26	63.4	352	1	1

New York	Att.	Comp.	Pct.	Yards	TDs	Int.
Simms	25	22	88.0	268	3	0

PASS RECEIVING

Denver	No.	Yards	Average	TDs
V. Johnson	5	121	24.3	1
Wilhite	5	39	7.8	0
Winder	4	34	8.5	0
M. Jackson	3	51	17.0	0
Watson	2	54	27.0	0
Sampson	2	20	10.0	0
Mobley	2	17	8.5	0
Sewell	2	12	6.0	0
Lang	1	4	4.0	0
Totals	26	352	13.5	1

New York	No.	Yards	Average	TDs
Bavaro	4	51	12.8	1
Morris	4	20	5.0	0
Carthon	4	13	3.3	0
Robinson	3	62	20.7	0
Manuel	3	43	14.3	0
McConkey	2	50	25.0	1
Rouson	1	23	23.0	0
Mowatt	1	6	6.0	1
Totals	22	268	12.2	3

S U P E R   B O W L   X X I

PUNTING

Denver	No.	Average	Long
Horan	2	41	42

New York	No.	Average	Long
Landeta	3	46	59

PUNT RETURNS

Denver	No.	Yards	Average
Wilhite	1	9	9.0

New York	No.	Yards	Average
McConkey	1	25	25.0

KICKOFF RETURNS

Denver	No.	Yards	Average
Bell	3	48	16.0
Lang	2	36	18.0

New York	No.	Yards	Average
Rouson	3	56	18.7
Flynn	1	−3	−3.0

INTERCEPTIONS

New York	No.	Yards
Patterson	1	−7